The Algerian Insurrection
1954–1962

by the same author

*

THE ARAB-ISRAELI WAR
THE SINAI CAMPAIGN, 1956
THE STORY OF THE FRENCH FOREIGN LEGION
THE RED ARMY
THE RED ARMY OF CHINA
THE INDO-CHINA WAR, 1945–54
THE GREEK CIVIL WAR, 1944–49
MALAYA: THE COMMUNIST INSURGENT WAR, 1948–60

The Algerian
Insurrection, 1954-62

EDGAR O'BALLANCE

ARCHON BOOKS
Hamden, Connecticut

*First edition published
in the United States
Archon Books
1967
Printed in Great Britain*

Contents

Maps

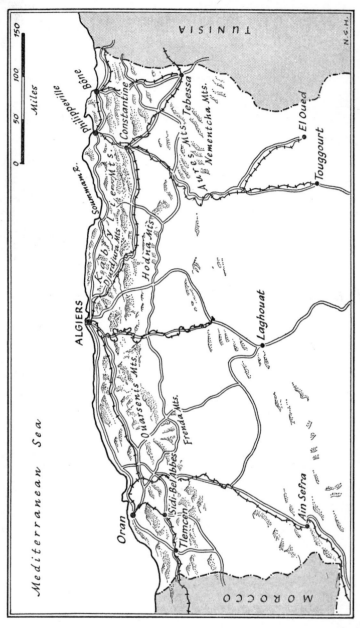

Algeria, showing some relief and communications

Preface

The Algerian Insurrection lasted from 1954 until 1962, when it was terminated by the Evian Agreements. It is the object of several misconceptions, and it is hoped this account may correct some of them. It is generally accepted that the outbreak of the rebellion took the French, the Europeans in Algeria and the Algerian Muslims by surprise, but it is not so well known that it was instigated and motivated by a small group of power-hungry, determined individuals who forced the Muslim population, initially by terrorist methods, to adopt and help further their programme. This was the seizure of total power, the ejection of the French and the subjugation of the Europeans in the country.

To those who had just mentally digested the Communist victory in China and the Viet Minh successes in French Indo-China, the outcome of the conflict in Algeria was never in doubt. They tended to assume that insurgent warfare, when carried out on a gigantic scale by a population against an alien government, had some magical properties that were proof against counter-action by conventional armies and military methods. Sometimes people wondered aloud why the French continued to fight on at all, and why they did not sink their pride and come to terms with the insurgents immediately. They did not realize that, far from losing the military battle, the French Army was winning it.

Such people had obviously insufficiently analysed the reasons for the Chinese and Viet Minh achievements, and had neglected to examine the real causes of lost insurgent and guerilla wars, such as those in Greece, the Philippines and Malaya. There are always many imponderables in any sort of war, the insurgent

9

type included, when vital omissions, neglects and mistakes can be, and are, made by both sides, often with far-reaching or even deadly results. Moreover, as in all human actions, chance in war plays a far greater part than most victorious generals and military historians are prepared to admit.

At the outset of hardly any war can either victory or defeat be guaranteed, as so many of these unforeseen and unpredictable factors are present and continue to appear on the scene as the struggle continues. The Algerian Insurrection was no exception. Far from being an easy, certain victory, as seems to be the general impression abroad nowadays, it was a hard struggle from the very beginning for the insurgents, who were plagued by internal dissensions, a rival nationalist organisation and a French Army that understood many anti-insurgent techniques. Operating underground, they had to form and expand an army, obtain arms and supplies, angle for international support and above all maintain morale in the face of French successes in the field, heavy casualties, desertions and faint-hearts.

The FLN leaders had planned to work to the, now better known, Communist insurgent blue-print, as drawn up by Mao Tse-tung and Ho Chi Minh, in which the struggle begins with a guerilla, or 'survival', phase, during which the insurgent army is established in mountain bases. It then moves on to the 'protracted' stage, the long-drawn-out test of strength and stamina in which Government forces should be harassed, dispersed and frustrated by 'hit-and-run' tactics, under cover of which a 'conventional' army is recruited, armed and trained. When this army is ready to flex its muscles and the Government forces are at their lowest ebb, the 'mobile' stage is embarked upon, in which the insurgent 'conventional' army practises large-scale movement about the country, still avoiding a head-on clash. The ultimate stage is that of a conventional battle, such as that at Dien Bien Phu, to inflict a military defeat on the Government army, after which there is no physical bar to the insurgents taking over power completely.

The FLN was not able to keep to this blue-print, as in the

PREFACE

military sphere the Algerian insurgents had few successes, and
often tried to jump impatiently from one stage in the progression to another before conditions were suitable. In 1959 they
were forced to revert from the protracted to the guerilla stage
of insurgent warfare, in order to survive, and during the last
months of the war, not only was the ALN in Algeria most definitely on the defensive, it was all but beaten. Outside Algeria,
effectively excluded by the electrified frontier barriers manned
by the French Army, lay in helpless idleness the 'conventional'
part of the ALN, originally formed, armed and trained to fight
the ultimate battle. It was never used.

On the French side lack of strong, stable government and
firm, wise handling of the Algerian problem in the early years
of the war, pressures from the Europeans in Algeria and other
factions, such as the French Communists and the Ultras, adverse world opinion and the fact that the French Army became
involved in politics, hamstrung their efforts to win a complete
victory, which on several occasions came far nearer to realisa-
tion than was apparent. Despite these handicaps, the French
Army contained the rebellion and much of the harsh, ill-
considered criticism directed against it is unjustified. It sealed
the frontiers almost completely, thus holding back impotently
a greater part of the insurgent army in both Morocco and
Tunisia, while inside Algeria it was winning the military battle
against the guerillas. By moving sections of the population it
deprived the insurgents of the support of the people, an essential
without which they cannot operate or live for long. On the
diplomatic side, the French managed to cut off the insurgents'
arms supplies.

With the guerilla mystique befogging many minds, the
Algerian insurgent army, both at the time and especially in
retrospect, has been excessively loaded with credit. It is true its
existence and activities contributed to the establishment of an
independent Algeria, but the ultimate victory was not gained
by a conventional battle, such as that at Dien Bien Phu, but
by political and diplomatic means.

This account of the course of the insurrection is not a long, exhaustive catalogue of all the bomb-throwing incidents, ambushes and armed clashes that took place, which would only weary and confuse, but it aims at giving a clear, broad picture of what really happened, with just enough precise detail to illustrate.

One must apologise for the many sets of initials that litter the text, but unfortunately these are necessary to avoid tedious repetition of long titles of organizations.

EDGAR O'BALLANCE

Glossary

Fidayines	=	village militia, usually unarmed insurgents
Moujahidines	=	the insurgent, uniformed, armed fighters of the ALN
Moussebilines	=	the insurgent regional militia, without uniforms and often without arms
Ulema	=	religious teachers
Wilaya	=	insurgent military-political-administrative region

Abbreviations

Unfortunately a number of abbreviations, usually sets of initials, are necessary to avoid a long and tedious repetition of the full titles of organizations and bodies. The following are the main ones used:

ALN = Armée de Libération Nationale (Army of National Liberation)

AML = Amis du Manifeste et de la Liberté (Friends of the Manifesto and Liberty)

CCE = Comité de Coordination et d'Exécution (Committee of Co-ordination and Execution)

CEMN = Comité d'Entente des Mouvements Nationaux (Agreement Committee of National Movements); known also as the 'Comité d'Entente'

CNRA = Conseil National de la Révolution Algérienne (National Council of the Algerian Revolution)

CRUA = Comité Révolutionnaire pour l'Unité et l'Action (Revolutionary Committee for Unity and Action)

DOP = Détachements Opérationnels de Protection (Army Psychological Detachments)

DST = Direction de la Surveillance du Territoire (French Security Police)

ENA = Etoile Norde Africaine (African North Star)

FEMA = Fédération des Elus Musulmans d'Algérie (Federation of Elected Muslims in Algeria)

FLN = Front de Libération Nationale (National Liberation Front)

GPRA = Gouvernement Provisoire de la République

	Algérienne (Provisional Government of the Algerian Republic)
MNA	= Mouvement National Algérien (Algerian National Movement
MRP	= Mouvement Républicain Populaire (Popular Republican Movement)
MTLD	= Mouvement pour le Triomphe des Libertés Démocratiques (Movement for the Triumph of Democratic Liberties)
OAS	= Organisation Armée Secrète (Secret Army Organization)
OPA	= Organisation Politico-Administrative (Political-Administrative Organization)
ORU	= Organisation Rurale et Urbaine (Rural and Urban Organization of FLN)
OS	= Organisation Secrète (Secret Organization)
OS	= Organisation Spéciale (Special Organization) of the MTLD
PCA	= Parti Communiste Algérien (Algerian Communist Party)
PPA	= Parti du Peuple Algérien (Party of the Algerian People)
RFMA	= Rassemblement Franco-Musulman Algérien (Rally of Algerian French Muslims)
RPF	= Rassemblement du Peuple Français (Rally of French People)
SAS	= Sections Administratives Specialisées (Special Administrative Section)
SAU	= Sections Administratives Urbaines (Urban Administrative Section)
UDMA	= Union Démocratique du Manifesto Algérien (Democratic Union of the Algerian Manifesto)
UGCA	= Union Générale des Commerçants et des Artisans (General Union of Algerian Tradesmen)
UGEMA	= Union Générale des Etudiants Musulmans Algériens (General Union of Algerian Muslim Students)

ABBREVIATIONS

UGTA   = Union Générale des Travailleurs Algériens (General Union of Algerian Workers)

UPA   = Union Populaire Algérienne (Popular Algerian Union)

USTA   = Union Syndicale des Travailleurs Algériens (Syndicated Union of Algerian Workers)

CHAPTER 1

Background to Insurrection

To follow the rise of nationalism in Algeria and the uneven, and at times surprising, course of the insurrection, which lasted from November 1954 until July 1962, it is necessary to describe briefly the people and the terrain, explain the French presence, and add a few historical notes to give the essential background against which events can be clearly seen and appreciated as they unfold.

The indigenous people of the northern part of what is now the independent state of Algeria were Berbers, fierce and warlike, who gave the Phoenicians, Romans, Vandals and Byzantines, successive invaders, a hard fight. In the seventh century, the Sword of Islam was brought by the Arabs, forcibly converting people to this new religion. The conversion of the Berbers to Mohammedanism was completed by another Arab invasion in the eleventh century. After this the Berbers generally withdrew into the mountainous areas, retaining a sort of semi-independence and their own language and customs, the conquering Arabs settling mainly along the coastal strip and on the plains. The Ottoman Turks were the next conquerors, coming to Algeria[1] in the sixteenth century. Algeria was then known merely as part of the Magreb (Mughrib), which simply meant the 'west'.

The following century, corsairs in the coastal region seized power from the Turkish-appointed Deys and Beys who ruled for the Ottoman Empire. The fortified city of Algiers became

[1] The name Algeria (Algérie) was first used in a French official document in 1839.

a notorious pirates' nest, and in their fast ships, rowed by slaves many of whom were Europeans, the corsairs preyed on the merchant shipping of all nations that ventured within their orbit. These activities gave that section of North Africa, the Barbary (Berber) Coast, an evil reputation. The word barbarian is derived from Berber.

Corsair depredations on their ships in the Mediterranean irritated European Powers, and in 1683, for example, a French fleet attacked and sacked Algiers. Other similar expeditions of a punitive nature were mounted over the years by other European nations, the Pope and even America, but, as they were not followed up, the pirates, who merely retired temporarily into the chaotic hinterland, were able to re-establish themselves and resume their nefarious activities when the danger had passed. The periodic presence of warships of various nations in the vicinity of the Algerian coastline tended to curb this piracy, but these measures were only a partial answer.

The dominance of the corsairs in the coastal region caused the power of Turkey to wane in Algeria, and although the Deys and Beys still ruled, nominally at least for Turkey, they had to employ mercenary soldiers, Janissaries, to support them. Later, the Turkish-appointed rulers became the pawns of their Janissaries, when Deys and Beys rose and fell, often in quick succession, as groups of Janissaries, and powerful or cunning individuals, jostled and schemed for authority, playing off one faction, group or tribe against another, at times using intrigues and bribes as much as force to gain, or retain, position. Algeria was something of a 'no man's land' on the outer fringe of the Ottoman Empire, beyond effective reach or control of Constantinople, forming a somewhat convenient, although seething and lawless, buffer territory between it and the rival Muslim Empire of Morocco, just to the west.

Roughly speaking, Algeria consists of three basic physical sectors. In the north is a fertile coastal strip, varying from about 50 to 100 miles in width, which has an attractively pleasant Mediterranean climate. Immediately to the south of it, running approximately parallel, is the chain of the Maritime Atlas

Mountains, the domain of the Berbers, which divides the coastal strip from the 'Tell', or plateau of rolling downland, not quite so fertile, that extends southwards to the Lesser Atlas Mountain ranges. South again from these mountains lies the Sahara (meaning in Arabic literally 'nothing') Desert, hot and arid, a large part of which is incorporated in present-day Algeria.

It was not so much a desire for colonial expansion as such that caused the French to mount an invasion of Algeria, but rather the thought that a grandiose victory on the Napoleonic style might divert attention from the growing unpopularity of Charles X's régime in France. The nominal cause of the dispute between France and Algeria was a protracted quibble with some Algerian Jewish traders to whom the French Government had owed large sums of money since Revolutionary days. The Dey of Algiers espoused the cause of his Jewish subjects, and, tired of receiving evasive answers, summoned the French Consul into his presence when, during the course of an unsatisfactory interview, he was alleged to have struck the Frenchman with (as most accounts say) a fly whisk.

This incident occurred in April 1827, but the quarrel took some time to fester, as the French invasion did not take place until three years later, when, on 14th June 1830, French troops landed on the coast some 25 miles from Algiers, taking that city about three weeks later after heavy fighting. Initially, the annexation of only part of the coastal zone seems to have been envisaged, and in the following months, apart from Algiers, only Bône and Oran were occupied. Charles X fell from power in the last days of July (1830), virtually leaving the French Expeditionary Force in Algeria without a positive policy. In face of fierce, continuous, active resistance, the army was forced for its own protection to enlarge its bridgeheads and to take other towns.

By 1840, when additionally Mostaganem, Arzew, Bougie and Constantine had been seized by force of French arms, it was obvious that the security of the French-occupied cities and towns depended upon the pacification of the countryside, and so hesitation and indecision were at last pushed aside and a policy of all-out conquest adopted. The conquest of Algeria by the French was no easy walk-over, but tough and hard fought, and it was not until 1857 that the whole country was physically occupied. Complete pacification was not accomplished until 1881.

In the meantime, right from the early 1830s, attempts were made to colonize Algeria with Frenchmen. Unemployed, undesirables and political unreliables were periodically shipped in batches to France's new overseas possessions to be settled on land taken from the Muslim inhabitants. It had been hoped that sufficient French people would be attracted to the idea of emigrating, but comparatively few could be persuaded to do so, and a policy of sponsoring and encouraging other Mediterranean races to come and settle in Algeria was instigated. In 1839, for example, there were some 25,000 European settlers in Algeria, but only 11,000 of them were French. The remainder were mainly Spanish, Maltese and Corsican. The army had set up an Arab Bureau to regulate settlers and conduct Arab affairs.

The inflow of European settlers continued spasmodically for the next 30 years or so. Perhaps the last large influx of those of French origin was from Alsace and Lorraine, who arrived after the Franco-German War of 1870. By 1874, there was a European community in Algeria of about 109,400, but only about 47,000 were French or of French origin.

These colonists, or 'Colons' as they came to be known, were given land. As early as 1844, the French Government claimed all undeveloped land unless any Muslim could show good title to it, and in the following year land belonging to any 'rebels' was also seized, to be parcelled out to the Colons. In 1872, after the last big Kabylie (Berber) Rebellion, one million acres of good land were confiscated for this purpose. From 1833 onwards, various Ordinances proclaimed that Algeria, or such areas of the country as were progressively effectively occupied, was to be considered to be part of Metropolitan France. When the supply of European colonists tailed off, expropriated land was given to large private investment companies in the hope that they would stimulate immigration and establish more settlements. Some attempts were made to curb land appropriation and to protect Muslims from land-sharks, but these were mostly either nullified or circumvented.

Farming the most fertile land in the country, the Colons concentrated upon cereal and wine production, obtaining subsidies from France to help develop them. Hard work and careful husbandry enabled many Colons to create large, prosperous farms, which were all too often in striking contrast to the lackadaisical, primitive agricultural efforts of the Muslim farmers. Non-French goods coming into Algeria were heavily taxed, as the idea was that the country should provide an outlet for the industrial products of France. Accordingly, few industries, and none of any magnitude, were established in Algeria in the nineteenth century, the accent being on encouraging the Colons to concentrate upon agriculture.

This policy began to change in the twentieth century, but owing to lack of cheap power, industry in Algeria did not develop to any great extent until after World War II, during which the French had come to realise the economic value of their North African possessions. Deposits of iron, lead, zinc, phosphates and other minerals were being exploited by 1954, when locally mined coal provided fuel for about 35 power stations. The search was on for oil and other resources in commercially workable quantities. By this time, communications had been developed to some extent, there being (in 1954) over 27,000 miles of first class and over 35,000 miles of other sorts of roads, and about 3,000 miles of railway, as well as 30 airports and six seaports with good harbour facilities. Many small industries, especially those making consumer goods, had been established and plans existed to set up more.

Still having a primarily agricultural economic base, Algeria had (in 1954) about 32 million acres of arable land, but owing to irrigation problems, only some $17\frac{1}{2}$ million acres could be cultivated by modern methods. Of this latter figure, about four million acres of the very best land was in possession of the Colons, or Europeans as they now preferred to be called. Other land worked or owned by Europeans may not have been quite so good, but it had invariably been improved and was well farmed.

The Muslim population began to increase[1] considerably in the twentieth century, outstripping its agricultural output by 1939, until by 1954 its estimated annual increase was about 250,000. Of the Muslim population, which was 8,451,000 in January 1954, the majority lived in rural conditions, mainly on small farms, often on marginal land. About three million of them were literally landless, while another million were so under-employed, as their own land would not yield sufficient for them to live upon, that they had to do casual work on European farms.[2] The French began a study of agricultural improvement for the Muslim farmers in 1937, but World War II interrupted this and it was not until 1949 that the first Four Year Plan to improve agriculture by soil conservation,[3] drainage and irrigation was started.

About 150,000 Algerian Muslims worked as labourers in France, their families in Algeria existing on the money they sent home. The first Algerian Muslims had gone to work in France in 1904 in the sugar refineries near Marseilles. Mass migration to France for this purpose did not begin until World War I, when about 150,000 went to work in factories. After 1918 only about 50,000 remained, and this number only slowly doubled to 100,000 by 1948, after which it increased at a faster pace.

Not only did the Muslims have the poorer land, but they were a long way behind in education, having an illiteracy rate (1954) of about 90 per cent, with only about 9 per cent being able to write. About 27 per cent of them spoke only Berber.

The presence of a mixed French-officered army made up of French volunteer units, the French Foreign Legion, Algerian,

[1] The population of Algeria in 1830 was thought to have been about 2 million. Official figures issued showed the population of the country at 1st January 1954 as being 9,530,000.

[2] Later, in 1961 for example, some figures issued by the Government showed that the average income of a Muslim farmer was only 3 per cent of that of a European farmer.

[3] About 100,000 acres of agricultural land was being lost annually by erosion.

Moroccan and Tunisian troops, and soldiers from other French territories, such as Senegal, discouraged any risings or revolts by discontented tribes.

The other community in Algeria, the Europeans, numbering about one million, were generally much better off than the Muslims, owning about 90 per cent of the industry and some 40 per cent of the best land in the country. Of this group, perhaps about 15,000 were 'gros Colons', who were the large landowners, senior civil servants and administrators, while at the other end of the scale were about 10,000 unskilled Europeans, who were labourers, and in fact, little better off than the average Muslim. In between these two extremes of wealth and poverty lay the bulk of the Europeans, who were school teachers, shopkeepers, business men, clerks and technicians. As a class the Europeans felt an inborn sense of superiority towards the Muslim, tinged with the background fear of being heavily outnumbered by the Muslim masses.

Racially divided and mutually suspicious, the Europeans and the Muslims were definitely two separate racial elements within the country, and each kept much to itself, each having its own customs, habits and way of life. The Europeans were educated, progressive, energetic and hard-working, while the Muslims were outwardly docile and resigned to their lot. The Europeans claimed they had made and developed Algeria, which was nothing before they came except a chaotic 'no man's land', alleging the Muslims had neglected or wasted opportunities through ignorance, prejudice or laziness.

Senior Government officials and administrators were almost all French, with French, as opposed to French-Algerian, background and traditions, and their first loyalties and thoughts were always directed towards France, rather than Algeria as a country. They tried to be impartial, but extracts from some of their reports reveal that they were impressed neither by the Algerian Muslims nor by the Europeans. French officers and soldiers serving in Algeria were of much the same view, with the possible exception of those serving with Algerian Muslim units, who often came to like and respect their soldiers.

CHAPTER 2

The Rise of Algerian Nationalism

During the first two decades of colonization the French broke up what could loosely be called the Arab middle class, and this did not begin to re-appear until the early twentieth century when a class of French-educated intellectuals, French-appointed Arab leaders and army officers started to materialize. The ambition of this rising middle class was complete integration with France, and the highest honour that could be gained was that of French citizenship, which was sparingly bestowed. This small group of Algerian Muslims looked to France as the fountain-head of their hopes and ambitions. As Muslims could only obtain this pearl of French citizenship if they gave up certain Islamic practices, they were slightingly referred to as the 'Beni Oui Oui', the 'Tribe of Yes-men'.

The Algerian population, both Arab and Berber, was kept in a state of docility by the semi-educated marabouts, or holy men, who functioned under French encouragement, and who, as they were invariably susceptible to French influence, were also known as Beni Oui Oui, or 'Yes-men'. France ruled as far as was possible, especially in the countryside, through the 'caids', or French-appointed tribal leaders, who were also regarded as Beni Oui Oui. At municipal and local level there was a lack of Muslim representation, where the Europeans were easily able to out-vote them. Muslims, even though they achieved French citizenship, did not have the same rights as the Europeans.

The Europeans, who, for example, by 1912 numbered about 800,000 out of a total population (then) of about four and a half million, had become organized and powerful enough, not only to make their voice heard, but to block unwanted and unpopular legislation and to nullify objectionable Governor-General's decrees. They had opposed Muslim conscription in 1914, but during World War I over 100,000 Algerian Muslim volunteers had fought in France. European opposition to concessions to Muslims grew more determined. In 1919, when Algeria was firmly considered to be part of Metropolitan France, an attempt was made to give Muslims full voting rights, but this was watered down to almost nothing under European pressures.

Until World War I the overriding authority of the Governors-General had diverted or diluted all Muslim attempts to become integrated with France. The French-educated Muslims were rejected by the Europeans, who looked down on them as Algerians who had ideas far above their appointed station in life. Nor were they fully accepted or trusted by their own people, and so had influence in neither camp.

Algerian national and political movements began to appear after World War I, and in the early 1920s a small Algerian Communist Party, the 'Parti Communiste Algérien', the PCA, was formed as an adjunct to the French Communist Party. The Comintern tried to exert its influence on infant Communist parties in many colonial countries, including Algeria, but the PCA, whose leaders were mainly Europeans, rejected the Comintern instruction to work for the 'liberation' of Algeria, as they considered such a course to be impracticable. On the other hand, the French Communist Party accepted the Comintern idea, and accordingly there arose a difference between the two almost affiliated Communist Parties, which continued for several years. It was not until 1934 that a serious attempt was made to try and heal this breach, when at the instigation of Moscow better liaison and understanding between the two was promoted.

Effective Communist influence, as directed from Moscow, was absent from the early Algerian political parties, although Algerian Communists either formed, or joined, them, and

Communist organization and methods were freely adopted. The PCA drew scant support from the Muslims, and perhaps this was the main reason why the Comintern failed to get a grip on the subversive political organizations of Algeria, as it succeeded in doing in some other countries.

One of the first political movements in Algeria was the 'Fédération des Elus Musulmans d'Algérie' (Federation of Elected Muslims in Algeria), sometimes referred to as the FEMA, which was composed almost entirely of French-educated intellectuals and former Muslim officers in French Army units. It wanted total integration, with complete French and Muslim political equality. The difference in rights and status between Muslim and European citizens was considerable. Although the FEMA included such later famous revolutionary figures as Ferhat Abbas and Ben Djelloul, it never gained mass Muslim support.

The second political movement in Algeria was the 'Etoile Norde Africaine' (African North Star), the ENA, which was formed on the outskirts of Paris in 1924 by Hadj Abdel Kader, a member of the Central Committee of the French Communist Party. There was a heartfelt cry from the Algerian Muslim workers in France for economic equality, which aspiring Algerian revolutionaries and politicians exploited. The ENA drew a majority of its members from Algerian workers in France. It wanted complete independence from France for Algeria, something never voiced before by Algerian politicians, and it also advocated economic and social reforms.

In 1927, the ENA accepted the leadership of Hadj Ben Ahmed Messali, also a Communist, more usually known as Messali Hadj, an Algerian Muslim, who had spent part of his youth in the Red industrial belt of Paris. These two first leaders gave a distinct Communist stamp to the organization. The PCA at this stage generally supported the Muslim nationalist movements in the country, although it was left to the Muslim Communists, of whom there were very few, to take positive action. The ENA gained popular support, both in Algeria and France, especially amongst the industrial workers, and when it was forcibly dissolved by the Government for the first time in 1929, it claimed some 4,000 active members. The ENA was revived again in 1933.

In 1935, the 'Association of Algerian Ulema' (religious teachers), known simply as the Ulema, was formed by Sheikh Abdel Hamid Ben Badis, and its objects were both Islamic and national. Generally, between the two World Wars, the Islamic religion played a major role and provided the unifying element in the rise and development of Algerian nationalism. The influence of Ulema quickly spread to the cities and towns in Algeria and then to the countryside where it undermined the authority of the French-sponsored marabouts. Its members were largely orthodox Muslims, who disliked French control over their religion.

The Ulema programme had three points in common with the ENA; these were: independence from France, opposition to French culture and the adoption of Arabic as the official language of Algeria. Acceptance of any one of these three basic points would have upset the status and rights of the Europeans, who began to bring what pressures they could against this organization. Also, this preaching of unity amongst Muslims through a religious medium, something that had not been done before in Algeria during the French occupation, invoked active French disapproval as it contravened the traditional colonial policy of 'divide and rule'.

In Paris, the response to these startling nationalistic demands varied, the conservative and business elements were against them, but the Liberals and the Left, including the French Communists, were generally in favour of Algerian equality and freedom within the French national framework. The views of the French Government of the time, together with the powers and pressures of the different lobbies in the Capital, were reflected in how much action, if any, was taken against the Algerian nationalists.

In 1936, the Popular Front Government of Blum introduced a proposal in the French National Assembly to extend French citizenship to over 20,000 Algerian Muslims. This was known as the 'Blum-Violette' plan[1] and it aroused considerable controversy. As a protest all the European mayors in Algeria resigned, and the measure was circumvented.

The French Communist Party, whose strategy at that moment demanded that it should dissociate itself from the cause of an independent Algeria, turned against the ENA. In January 1937, the ENA was officially dissolved by the Popular Front Government, but by March, Messali Hadj had cunningly transformed it into the 'Parti du Peuple Algérien' (Party of the Algerian People), the PPA, which put forward similar demands, but in a milder way.

Messali Hadj publicly broke with the French Communists and all traces of Marxist ideology disappeared from his programme. Instead, he became an advocate of Pan-Arabism. The PPA became a nationalist party with a strong working class following, both in France as well as Algeria, that supported Islamic ideals.

The unrewarding association with the various French political parties brought only frustration. Differences of opinion arose between the several Algerian Muslim nationalist leaders over methods, causing both splintering and fusion of the movements. In 1938, Ben Djelloul broke away from the intellectual FEMA and formed his own party, the 'Rassemblement Franco-Musulman Algérien' (Rally of Algerian French-Muslims), the RFMA. This had an independent nationalist programme that called for the suppression of those French laws in Algeria that mitigated against the equality of the Muslims and the Europeans.

Ferhat Abbas also left the FEMA to form his own party, the 'Union Populaire Algérienne' (Popular Algerian Union), the UPA. This was not so extremist in character as the RFMA, and stood for the evolution of Muslims within the French national framework. Ferhat Abbas had always been an integrationist, and had at one time openly declared that there was no foundation for Algerian nationalism, since historically Algeria had never existed as a nation until after the arrival of the French.

Thus in 1939, the situation was that the PPA, the Ulema and

[1] Violette was a former Governor-General of Algeria.

the RFMA were working for Algerian independence, while the UPA favoured reform within the French national framework. On the outbreak of World War II, both the PPA and the Ulema were officially suppressed. The seemingly more moderate RFMA was left alone for the time being. The PPA went underground and continued to function as a political organization, although most of its leaders were detained.

After the Fall of France in 1940, the hand of the Vichy Government rested heavily on Algeria, which was under its control. All Algerian political parties were banned and many political leaders imprisoned. The Vichy Government paid more attention to the wishes and demands of the Europeans, and generally the Muslims lost many of the advantages and benefits they had gained over the years. The Vichy Government was most unsympathetic towards Algerian nationalist aspirations, being perhaps too weak to be generous and too unsure of itself to be magnanimous. Ferhat Abbas, who remained at liberty, being considered a moderate, made several overtures, but all were coldly rejected. This caused him to change his political convictions. Until this time he had been pro-French in every way, and had worked merely to persuade the French to give all Muslims in Algeria French citizenship on equal terms with the Europeans. Now his thoughts switched to Algerian autonomy.

The Allied landings in North Africa in November 1942 broke the Vichy Government hold over Algeria; and, although it did not include any Free French elements, a Free French Provisional Government was established by the Allies in North Africa. Soon afterwards, when the Free French sought to enlist the aid of the Algerian Muslims in continuing the war against the Axis Powers, they were abruptly faced by the Algerian Manifesto. This document was presented by Ferhat Abbas, who had drawn it up in collaboration with the PPA and the Ulema: in brief, it demanded a federal solution for Algeria with complete autonomy as a pre-condition of full participation in the war.

Ferhat Abbas had been influenced by the Atlantic Charter,

the American attitude towards the emancipation of colonial territories, the military defeat and weakness of France, the loss of French prestige in Muslim eyes and the inflexible attitude of the Europeans. The Algerian Manifesto, signed by Ferhat Abbas and 27 other Muslim elected members of local assemblies, was produced in February 1943 and handed to the French Governor-General the following month. A Supplementary (additif), with increased Muslim demands, was presented by other Arab and Kabylie leaders a few months afterwards.

On 3rd June 1943, General de Gaulle and General Giraud became the co-chairmen of the French Committee of National Liberation, which brushed aside the Algerian Manifesto with vague promises and other sops. In December, General de Gaulle announced that certain categories of Muslims could become French citizens without renouncing their Muslim status. In March 1944, voting rights were granted to most male adult Muslims, though for a separate college, and the proportion of Muslim representatives in local assemblies was slightly increased, although it still left the Europeans in the great majority. But none of these condescending measures gave satisfaction.

The virtual rejection of the Algerian Manifesto caused Ferhat Abbas to organize the 'Amis du Manifeste et de la Liberté' (Friends of the Manifesto and Liberty), the AML, to work for autonomy and social reforms, but still within the French political framework. Political parties were allowed to function again openly, and the AML membership ultimately rose to about 500,000. The revived PPA, however, had reservations about the moderate AML programme, instead advocating direct action in the countryside as being the only way to achieve independence from the French.

Ferhat Abbas still favoured peaceful means and was heartened by American pressures in persuading Colonial Powers, including France, to grant independence to colonial territories. Syria and the Lebanon became independent in 1943, for example, and they were encouraging precedents. He hoped for peaceful evolution but all Algerian leaders did not agree with him. About this period several attempts were made to unite the various nationalist parties, but these failed owing to disagreements between those who wanted revolution and those who were content with evolution. Ferhat Abbas represented those who favoured non-violent evolution. His old desire for integration had become heavily overshadowed by that for autonomy. Despite the slightly relaxed conditions, few Muslims now strove to become French citizens.

On VE Day, 8th May 1945, an Algerian nationalist procession in the town of Setif clashed with the police. Shots were fired and some Europeans and Muslims were killed. That night armed Muslims roamed the district, killing, looting and burning. Altogether, about 100 Europeans lost their lives. The authorities stepped in swiftly and harshly put down what they thought to be a nationalist rising. Official estimates of the killed in the punitive repression were about 1,500, but other estimates given rose to the 40,000 mark. There were also riots in Kabylie at the same time, which were ruthlessly suppressed, and it is thought that in all about 10,000 Muslims lost their lives as the result of them at the hands of the army, the police or groups of Europeans. After this, the PPA, which was thought to have organized the Setif incidents, was banned.

The European-controlled Algerian Communist Party, the PCA, denounced the Setif incident as Fascist inspired, and its members took part in the brutal suppression. The French Government that ordered these reprisals contained two Communists, Maurice Thorez and Charles Tillon.

When he realized that the PPA had been implicated in the violent Setif Incident, Ferhat Abbas organized the 'Union Démocratique du Manifesto Algérien' (Democratic Union of the Algerian Manifesto), the UDMA, which advocated an autonomous Algeria federated to France. The UDMA, which superseded the AML, attracted many French-educated Muslims from the professional classes, but gained little mass support.

In June 1946, Messali Hadj was released from detention to find his old PPA driven underground. Now a convinced Pan-Arabist, in November of that year he formed the 'Mouvement Pour le Triomphe des Libertés Democratiques' (Movement for the triumph of Democratic Liberties), the MTLD. The MTLD was virtually the revived PPA, and its members consisted mainly of workers, with some students and intellectuals. Many were disgruntled or had grievances, real or imaginary, and most had a tendency to take to violence, which led in many instances to imprisonment or banishment. In turn, these caused the MTLD to be secretive in its methods.

The MTLD stood for much more than simply autonomy for Algeria, and its programme included universal suffrage, the removal of French control over religion and schools, and the evacuation of French troops from the country. Most MTLD resolutions were in favour of complete independence and were against federal status.

In March 1947, it was decided at the first MTLD Congress, not without argument, not to form a para-military force for the time being, but instead to press for reform openly and non-violently. There was a degree of liaison and co-operation between the MTLD and the UDMA, and now both officially renounced direct action as a means of achieving their aims, concentrating their efforts on winning as many seats as possible at the local elections, where they had some success. Both organizations had adopted a Communistic framework and employed many Communist political methods.

Uneasy and unsettled politics in France were reflected in Algeria and in the handling of Algerian problems. In September 1947, the controversial Algerian Statute was passed by the French National Assembly, which pleased neither the Algerian Muslims nor the Europeans. It discarded the idea of integration and recognized two separate communities in Algeria, the Muslims and the Europeans, both within the French Union. It also created a new Algerian Assembly, elections for which were to be held in April 1948.

It was estimated that the majority of the Muslims were under the influence of the MTLD, or were sympathetic to its aims, as this organization gained fairly wide support in the cities and towns, and that accordingly the new Algerian Assembly would have a majority of Muslim representatives. European anxiety at this prospect was great and all pressures possible were brought to bear to avoid such a result. In short, the elections were almost blatantly rigged. The Governor-General, Naegelen, was afterwards blamed for this. The later elections of 1951 and 1953 were similarly 'arranged'.

This manipulation of the ballot box gave fuel for those Algerian nationalists who wanted direct action, and a clandestine para-military force, known as the 'Organisation Spéciale' (Special Organization), the OS, was created within the MTLD. Composed of active militants, dedicated to the use of violence and force to gain independence, the first leader of the OS was Hocine Ait Ahmed.

Mohammed Ben Bella took over the leadership of the OS early in 1950, when its governing committee consisted of himself and three regional commanders, each of whom directed and co-ordinated OS activities within their own regions. The OS had co-opted Mohammed Khider, a Muslim Deputy in the French National Assembly, as an adviser on political matters.

However, in March (1950), the existence of the OS, which had expanded to a probable strength of about 1,800, was discovered by the authorities and arrests were made. The problem of whether or not to continue to support the OS produced a split within the MTLD that hindered Party activity and progress for some time. This split was exacerbated by the fact that the Central Committee of the MTLD took exception to Messali Hadj's pursuit of the 'personality cult'. The unearthing of the OS broke the alliance between the UDMA and the MTLD. After some indecision, the MTLD formally dissolved the OS and officially denounced the use of force as a means of obtaining its objectives. Many OS members took refuge in Egypt, where the headquarters of the Arab League, which had espoused the Algerian nationalists' cause, functioned, while others went to France secretly or to Middle East or Muslim countries.

The lack of French response to moderate demands tended to draw nationalists together, and in 1951, the Central Committee of the MTLD formed an alliance with the UDMA, the Ulema, and the PCA, which had a brief life being known as the 'Algerian Front for the Defence and Respect of Liberty'. This decision was opposed by Messali Hadj, the leader of the MTLD, who regarded this action by his Central Committee as a threat to his leadership and a danger to his position, so he undertook a personal speaking tour of Algeria to assert his personal authority and prestige, which stirred up incidents and caused clashes between the factions within his Party. Eventually, in May 1952, Messali Hadj was deported from Algeria for subversive activities and detained in France.

The increasing influence and pressure of the Europeans and the efforts of the French authorities in Algeria had not succeeded in strangling the nationalist organizations or smothering their aspirations, but had merely magnified the difference between the two communities to the extent that the door was fast closing on the possibility of negotiation and peaceful evolution.

Economically 1952 was a better year for the French, and enabled them, with the American assistance received, to continue the disastrous war in Indo-China, which was naturally being very closely watched by Algerian nationalists of all shades of opinion. It was also the year in which subversive violence began in neighbouring Tunisia and Morocco, which steadily increased in tempo until it eventually led to both countries gaining their independence from France in 1956. This process was also carefully studied by the Algerian nationalists, especially those who advocated direct action.

The Egyptian-based Arab League had created a 'Magreb Office', with an Algerian Section, to give support to the Algerian nationalist movements, and there were reports of Algerians being given military and subversive training in Middle East countries. There may not have been much substance in these reports, but certainly Algerian revolutionaries were welcome in Egypt, where they were given some assistance. The main efforts of the Magreb Office about this time were directed to helping Tunisian and Moroccan insurgents, but the Algerian cause was by no means neglected.

The following year (1953) was one in which the growing dissatisfaction of the militant elements within the political parties began to be felt. Many of the more fiery revolutionaries left Algeria, either in disgust or to make preparations for more active and positive measures, and Cairo became their Mecca. The split in the MTLD remained, with Messali Hadj, who had been released from detention, at loggerheads with his Central Committee. On 15th July 1954, Messali Hadj convened a MTLD Congress in Belgium, which voted him full powers. As a counter, the Central Committee, feeling that a revolutionary party should have collective leadership, called a MTLD Congress in Algiers on 13th August. This gave the Central Committee full power of action. Thus there arose two opposing factions within the MTLD, the Messalists and the Centralists.

At the Algerian Section of the Magreb Office of the Arab League, an Algerian, Mohammed Khider,[1] a former Deputy in the French National Assembly and former general-secretary of the PPA, had become the most influential personality. But when Nasser came to power in Egypt in November 1954, he favoured Ben Bella.[2] This may have been because Ben Bella was an Arab, as opposed to the several prominent Berber revolutionaries in Cairo at the time. Nasser was primarily interested in promoting Pan-Arabism of his own brand with himself as the sole leader. Two other powerful revolutionary Algerian figures in Cairo were Mohammed Boudiaf and Belkacem Krim, the latter a Kabylie. All four, who came to form the Algerian revolutionary leadership in exile at this stage, had been members of the underground OS.

After several unsuccessful attempts by this group to reconcile the two factions within the MTLD, Boudiaf called a meeting at Berne, Switzerland, in March 1954, which was attended by many former members of the OS and other Algerian nationalists who favoured direct action. From this meeting emerged

[1] Mohammed Khider, who had been in the illegal OS, had fled to Egypt in 1950 just as his immunity as a deputy was about to be lifted.
[2] Ben Bella had also been in the illegal OS and been imprisoned for this reason in 1950. He escaped in 1952 and went to Egypt.

a militant secret organization known as the 'Comité Révolutionnaire pour l'Unité et l'Action' (Revolutionary Committee for Unity and Action), the CRUA, the central committee of which consisted of nine members,[1] who are often referred to as the 'historic leaders' of the Algerian revolution. These nine are also sometimes called the 'Club des Neuf' (Club of Nine) and they are also known as the 'Mouadjahed', or Freedom Fighters.

Former members of the OS, many from Egypt and other Middle East countries, joined CRUA. Prominent revolutionaries and agitators were not accepted, as they were already known to the French and Algerian police and would have attracted unwelcome attention to the new organization. Switzerland[2] became the main CRUA centre, partly because it was close to France and also perhaps because some Algerians were beginning to resent increasing Egyptian interference and supervision. CRUA members living in France and elsewhere abroad were ordered to return to Algeria to be on the ground ready for action and to renew their contacts. Nasser assigned two Egyptian army officers to help CRUA formulate a plan to launch a general insurrection in Algeria. By early July Algeria was divided into Wilayas, or military districts, and the commanders nominated.

The CRUA made further attempts, during August and September, to reconcile the two factions within the MTLD[3] so that the revolution could be launched with united support, but none was successful. Eventually, at a meeting held in Switzerland, on 10th October, CRUA decided to carry on with its plan alone, which was to launch a military insurrection beginning on 1st November 1954.

---

[1] The founder members of the 'Club des neuf' were:

Mohammed Boudiaf	Mohammed Khider	Larbi Ben M'Hidi
Mohammed Ben Bella	Hocine Ait Ahmed	Mourad Didouche
Belkacem Krim	Rabat Bitat	Mustapha Ben Boulaid.

[2] The Swiss Government was unaware of these activities.

[3] The MTLD claimed to have some 14,000 members at this stage.

CHAPTER 3

The First Twenty Months

(November 1954—August 1956)

The Algerian Insurrection broke out suddenly, violently and unexpectedly on the night of 31st October/1st November 1954, when there were some 70 incidents of ambushing, bomb-throwing, attacks on police stations and buildings, arson and destruction. Generally these were scattered widely across the breadth of the country, but the greatest incidence occurred in the eastern part of Algeria, particularly in the Aures Mountains areas. They were carried out by small groups of revolutionary fighters, crudely armed with old rifles, shot-guns, home-made explosives and incendiary bombs. In all, seven Europeans were killed, several more wounded and a great deal of material damage done. It is difficult to assess the exact number of insurgent fighters[1] in action on this initial occasion, or how many helped them, directly or indirectly, in some way, but most estimates place it at between 2,000 and 3,000, of whom only a small proportion had fire-arms.

Surprise was complete. 1st November was All Saints' Day, a public holiday. The French authorities were astonished and dumbfounded, so were the Europeans and the Muslim masses, so were the Ulema, the UDMA and the PCA, and so were the trade unionists and other nationalists of all shades and views. The CRUA leadership had neither consulted, nor confided in, any of them.

The relatively quiet years since 1945, especially in the face

[1] The insurgent fighters became known to the French as 'Fellaga', meaning literally 'highwaymen'.

of active nationalist agitation in neighbouring Morocco and Tunisia, had lulled the French authorities into complacent smugness, and possible disloyalty of the Muslim population in Algeria had not occurred to them. In fact, at first it was more than suspected that the initial incidents in the eastern part of Algeria had been committed by bands of armed Tunisian nationalists from over the border, anxious to stir up trouble to divert French attention from the insurgency problem in Tunisia at the time. The Tunisian and Moroccan struggles for independence, clandestinely supported by Egypt and other Arab countries, were reaching their climax. Wedged between restless Morocco and Tunisia, Algeria had seemed surprisingly placid.

The French military command in Algeria thought it was probably a small tribal revolt in the Aures and Kabylie Mountains, or an unconnected series of them, and immediately four battalions of paratroops and several companies of security troops were sent over from France as reinforcements. The Aures Mountains rise to a height of about 5,000 feet and are intersected by deep gorges, being the traditional refuge of rebels and bandits. A fairly large-scale police operation had been carried out in this area in 1952.

The Muslim masses neither knew the identity nor the aims of the insurgents, and they watched the initial, and successive, incidents with uncomprehending curiosity. Ferhat Abbas and his UMDA condemned the insurgents publicly, as did the Ulema and the PCA. On 5th November, the French Prime Minister, Mendès-France, said firmly that Algeria was part of the Republic and that there would be no compromise with sedition. As the pattern of revolt became more obvious, it was blamed on to criminal elements, who were allegedly stirred into foolish activity by professional agitators, the stress for discontent being placed on economic and social causes, but never put down to disloyalty, or dislike of French rule.

The French, rather unjustly, blamed the fragmented MTLD to some extent, and officially dissolved the organization. The police arrested hundreds of known or suspected terrorists, agitators and nationalists. In the countryside, in eastern Algeria, aircraft dropped leaflets over the badly affected areas, mainly in the Aures and Kabylie Mountains, urging the inhabitants to move into French-protected zones, so that they would be out of the danger area when the French Army began pacification measures. There was little or no response to this appeal, and by the end of the month, French troops, of whom there were about 60,000 in Algeria at the time, were moving against insurgent fighters in the mountains, and French aircraft bombed suspected insurgent concentrations. Helicopters were used to coordinate these operations right from the beginning.

As soon as the insurrection was launched, the CRUA leadership elements changed the name of their revolutionary organization to the 'Front de Libération Nationale' (the National Liberation Front), the FLN, so as to give an impression of unity. Having no obligation to any of the existing nationalist parties or groups, the leaders were in a strong, independent position. It was true that Ferhat Abbas had visited Cairo in July (1954), but he played no part in the initial insurgency, and neither had he any influence with CRUA.

Formerly, the controlling committee of CRUA, the original 'Club of Nine', had combined the political and military planning of the insurrection, but from 1st November it was decided to separate these two functions, and there came into being on this date the External Delegation and the Internal Delegation. The External Delegation, based on Cairo, and consisting of Ben Bella, Mohammed Khider, Mohammed Boudiaf and Hocine Ait Ahmed, controlled the political direction of the revolutionary movement, and was responsible for such matters as procuring arms and supplies, establishing lines of supply into Algeria, and obtaining diplomatic, financial and military assistance from any sympathetic states.

The Internal Delegation consisted of the nominated leaders of the Wilayas, the military zones or districts, in Algeria itself, who were the almost autonomous military commanders on the spot. These military leaders were concerned primarily with raising, arming and training a field force of insurgent fighters and supporting auxiliaries, and of pursuing active operations.

From 1st November, the insurgents in Algeria were officially known as the 'Armée de Libération Nationale' (Army of National Liberation), the ALN.

Copying the MTLD pattern, Algeria had already been divided into six Wilayas, intended to be combined military provinces and administrative areas, but initially only five commanders were nominated,[1] and during the opening months of the insurrection the recruiting, organization and growth of the ALN were left entirely in their hands. They had to form, build and train an armed force from their own resources as best they could. The Wilaya commanders named their own subordinates, and it depended upon their individual personality, skill, initiative and energy how effective, or otherwise, their own portion of the ALN became. The degree of success varied from Wilaya to Wilaya, and as liaison and co-operation between Wilayas were virtually non-existent, they sank or swam by their own efforts alone.

In the early stages small insurgent units were mainly involved in spasmodic, unco-ordinated, hit-and-run tactics, the chief object of which was to seize arms, ammunition and explosives. As confidence and experience were gained, and more fighters recruited and armed, so the size of the unit began to swell. Guerilla principles — such as never fighting unless sure of success and of always dispersing before greater or equal numbers of regular troops — were applied, to such an extent that it was obvious that many of the insurgent warfare lessons brought out in Red China and French Indo-China had been taken to heart very seriously.

After establishing a core of trained and indoctrinated fighters, expansion of the ALN tended to be limited by lack of arms, but despite this personnel continued to be recruited, often on a part-time basis to work as civilian auxiliaries in a supplying and supporting role. No potential recruit was turned down. On 1st November, the ALN had called for men between the ages of 18 and 40 years to volunteer but to remain at home until

[1] France was also divided into seven autonomous Wilayas for revolutionary purposes.

called forward. The auxiliaries, who included a few women, were taught to identify French units so as to be able to pass on valuable intelligence to the Wilaya commanders at all times. Other tasks included: moving ahead of ALN patrols and units to give warning of French troops, ambushes and patrols; courier duties; carrying, obtaining and storing supplies and smuggling arms and ammunition.

The six Wilayas in Algeria were:

Wilaya I: Based on the Aures Mountains, commanded by Mustapha Ben Boulaid.

Wilaya II: Based on the North Constantine region, commanded briefly by Rabah Bitat, and then by Mourad Didouche.

Wilaya III: Based on the Kabylie region, commanded by Belkacem Krim.

Wilaya IV: Based on the region just south of Algiers, which city it initially included, commanded briefly by Mourad Didouche, and then by Rabah Bitat.

Wilaya V: Consisted of most of Western Algeria, commanded by Larbi Ben M'Hidi.

Wilaya VI: Consisted of the territory to the south of Wilayas III and IV, and all the Sahara Desert. For the time being this was very much in the planning stage, and no commander was nominated by the FLN.

The first twenty months of the insurrection was a period of driving, energetic, disorganized confusion for the infant ALN, a period of trial and error, and then of gathering momentum. The Wilayas seemed to come to life one by one, to essay a few hit-and-run raids, usually with disastrous results to the aspiring guerillas, after which they were forced to withdraw their armed insurgents to safe areas to consolidate. For the ALN this was a testing period of the guerilla struggle for existence, before it had persuaded and terrorized the Muslim population into support-ing the FLN and its cause. These early months were difficult and trying, during which several leaders were killed or captured and internal struggles for military supremacy took place. It was not until January 1956, a full 14 months after the insurrection had been launched, when units in Wilaya V took to derailing trains on the Oran to Sidi Bel Abbes line, that it could be said that the ALN had effectually spread across the whole of northern Algeria.

The foremost and liveliest Wilaya was that commanded by Ben Boulaid, based on the Aures Mountains, who started off with about 150 armed men, divided into small groups. For several weeks he initiated numerous raids on police posts, ambushed French army patrols and wrought destruction on European farms, but vigorous French military counter-action caused Ben Boulaid to hastily withdraw the remnants of his force back into the depths of the Aures Mountains to avoid complete destruction.

In the comparative safety of the mountains, he organized a small guerilla army, which included command, intelligence and liaison sections. Numbers increased, but the supply of arms remained a problem, so he contacted two nomadic bandit groups on the fringe of the Sahara Desert and used them to smuggle in arms and other supplies for his men from Egypt, by way of south Libya, through Saharan oases and then north to the Aures Mountains. Although Ben Boulaid continued to carry out a few hit-and-run raids mainly to obtain arms, and undertook a few bomb-throwing terrorist incidents to show he was still active, it was not until April 1955 that this guerilla force felt strong and confident enough once again to embark on active guerilla operations against the, by this time, strengthened French forces.

In the meantime, on 11th February 1955, when on his way to see Ben Bella in Cairo about more supplies for his men, Ben Boulaid had been captured[1] by the French in southern Tunisia. His abrupt removal from command of Wilaya I, which had a growing, virile fighting force for which he should be given full

---

[1] A document alleged to have been found on Ben Boulaid at the time of his arrest indicated that his combat strength was 356 men. This might have meant armed and trained fighters, he would have several times that number of auxiliaries.

credit, was followed by disagreement amongst his subordinates (of whom there were about a dozen, each commanding a small detachment of insurgent fighters) as to who should succeed him. Eventually Bahir Chihani was nominated by the FLN as the commander, but he was unable to control the jealousies and rivalries within this section of the ALN. Also, not being a native of the Aures Mountains, as had been Ben Boulaid, he was not able to obtain such good co-operation and support from the local people. In addition, he was handicapped by the intrigues of Omar Ben Boulaid, Ben Boulaid's brother, who considered that he should, as a right, have been nominated commander in his brother's stead.

Supplies were always a problem in Wilaya I, as the clandestine routes were unreliable, and shortages of arms, ammunition and equipment became acute. More important, the insurgents became short of food and Bahir Chihani was forced to demand that the local population should feed his men. He also levied taxes. These actions were resented, and to enforce them Bahir Chihani resorted to traditionally cruel Berber punishments for non-co-operation, such as cutting off lips and noses.

Guerilla operations against the French were resumed in April 1955, but although restricted to 'mosquito' tactics—quickly striking and then rapidly withdrawing—losses were high and failures many, although of course, these activities caused French and European casualties and damage to property. An uneasy summer, during which little went right in Bahir Chihani's Wilaya, culminated in a rough court martial. The blame for all shortcomings and failures in the Wilaya was laid at his door by his subordinates, and Bahir Chihani was executed by them in October. It is easy to criticize Bahir Chihani for lack of leadership and military ability, but Wilaya I was under heavy French military pressure all the time he was in command; so perhaps, not being a native of the Aures Mountain region as most were, he was a convenient and acceptable scapegoat. In the guerilla survival stage of insurgent warfare only the shrewdest and toughest remain alive, let alone get to the top and stay there.

The ALN in Wilaya I was in a groggy way, when in November (1955) Ben Boulaid escaped from prison. Back in command, he took urgent and ruthless steps to put his slightly demoralized guerilla force in good order again. There were several executions and changes of subordinates. He then spent the remainder of the winter in recruiting, seizing arms and training his men ready for a spring offensive. However, a guerilla leader's life is always in danger, sometimes from his own organization as well as from the authorities he is fighting, and on 27th March 1956, Ben Boulaid was killed by a booby-trapped radio in his own command headquarters. Whether this had been done by a jealous rival, as part of a blood feud for executions he had ordered amongst the Aures Mountain natives, or by a counter-guerilla, is not known. But by this time the ALN in Wilaya I was fairly firmly established in the Aures Mountains. After his death, Omar Ben Boulaid became the self-appointed commander of the Wilaya.

The adjoining Wilayas II (the North Constantine region) and III (the Kabylie region) each started with a small, hard core of insurgent fighters, who in the opening weeks of the revolt undertook numerous hit-and-run raids in an attempt to relieve pressure from the Aures Mountains Wilaya, against which French troops were concentrating. These activities involved heavy losses, and when it became a question of survival or extinction, under a weak façade of guerilla, ambush and terrorist actions, the insurgents withdrew into more remote territory to concentrate upon consolidation, expansion and obtaining supplies.

It was the summer of 1955 before either Wilaya felt capable of attempting to put into effect the prescribed FLN strategy, which was a reversal of Marshal Lyautey's famous 'Tache d'Huile', or 'grease-spot' tactics. Lyautey's colonial strategy was to put down concentrations of troops in a population centre, and when that was brought under control, to slowly spread outwards into the surrounding countryside. The ALN strategy was to set up guerilla bases in the mountains, and then to slowly seep towards, and then into, the cities and towns.

When Mourad Didouche, the commander of Wilaya II, was killed in combat in January 1955, he was replaced by Youssef Zighout, who specialized in quick attacks and rapid withdrawals. Youssef Zighout, like other ALN commanders, concentrated upon seizing arms, and usually timed his ambushes for late afternoon, so that his fighters would have the cover of darkness all night to make good their escape in any subsequent search.

In the spring of 1955, Belkacem Krim, a Kabylie, the commander of Wilaya III (the Kabylie Mountain region), together with his deputy, Amar Ouamrane, moved his headquarters into the city of Algiers. Both men were former non-commissioned officers in the French Army. Communication between the Wilayas and the External Delegation was difficult, slow and unreliable, and so Belkacem Krim's chief political officer, Ramdane Abbane, recently released from a French prison in which he had been for revolutionary activities, made direct contact with the External Delegation in Cairo. Ramdane Abbane also did liaison work with other Wilayas. A good organizer, he was one of the few intellectuals of the insurrection. In this way, Belkacem Krim, through his political officer, Ramdane Abbane, became one of the most important and influential personalities in the ALN in Algeria.

In Wilaya III, Belkacem Krim had established a three-man committee in many of the villages to control them for the ALN. This consisted of a political agent who was responsible for recruiting and supporting the ALN generally, a tax collector and a civil affairs officer. Belkacem Krim did not hesitate to use terrorism to gain the required support and to persuade the people to do as he demanded, although he admitted that this method was not desirable.

Wilaya IV, commanded by Rabah Bitat, had a somewhat similar initial existence to the others, and apart from a few disjointed guerilla and terrorist tactics, little was done except to concentrate upon survival and consolidation. Rabah Bitat was captured by the French police in February in a café in Algiers, where he was waiting to meet Belkacem Krim. Rabah Bitat was replaced as commander of Wilaya IV by Amar Ouamrane. In June Amar Ouamrane was assisted by Ben Khedda, who had been released from prison.

Operations did not really begin in Wilaya V, the western part of Algeria, until September 1955, when Sultan Mohammed V returned to Rabat from exile. The headquarters of Wilaya V then moved to Oudjda, near the Moroccan border, from Nador in (then) Spanish Morocco. In December, Larbi Ben M'Hidi, the commander, visited Cairo, and on his return journey was arrested by the police in the Constantine region. Two days later he was reported to have been found dead in his cell.[1]

Back in Wilaya V, Abdul Hafid Boussouf, who had former Communist affiliations, was appointed by the FLN to command, and setting to work with energy and ability, he soon had a capable force of some 3,000 armed and trained fighters, whose equipment included machine-guns, automatic weapons and radios. This rapidly became the largest and most effective ALN force inside Algeria, causing the French Army to hastily commence building an electrified fence along part of the Moroccan frontier to prevent supplies reaching it and to stop infiltration.

In February 1956, a section of the Wilaya V ALN force fought a satisfactory engagement with French troops, giving as good as it got, and a month later it practically besieged the city of Tlemcen. This completed the effective spread of the ALN right across the northern part of the country. The active military insurgent movement had seeped westwards along the two mountain ranges that stretch across the northern part of Algeria, the Maritime Atlas and the Greater Atlas ranges, and then tentacled into other mountain ranges sprouting from them.

To the south, Wilaya VI was still little more than a dormant embryo.

---

[1] On 6th March 1957 the French officially said that Larbi Ben M'Hidi had hanged himself, but some French press reports indicated that he was secretly shot to avoid a public trial.

It is difficult to determine the initial strength of the ALN with any degree of accuracy, or to chart its early expansion systematically, partly because there was difficulty in differentiating between actual insurgent fighters, the auxiliaries and other supporters, partly because not all the so-called 'rebels' were in arms against the French Government for political reasons, and partly because certain revolutionary factions had not joined the ALN. Berber tribal leaders, for example, were deeply engrossed in feuds, and several nominally either joined the insurgents, or declared for the French, with the sole object of obtaining arms for their own private uses.

Other groups followed a similar course to allow themselves the means to indulge in banditry or large-scale smuggling for personal profit. However, this worked both ways and was frequently taken advantage of by the ALN, which, to gain the support of certain tribes or groups, combined with them to help defeat their tribal or group enemies. Both tribes and groups, and the ALN, were able to practise such activities because many of the mountainous parts of Algeria were under-administered and had been neglected (provided taxes were paid) by Government officials for years. Many villages in the mountains had not seen a French administrator for a decade or more.

Assuming that the figure of about 3,000 insurgent fighters was correct in November 1954—which it may have been—it is thought that this number only slowly rose to the 5,000 mark, and that it was not until the winter of 1955–56, when the ALN gave serious attention to expansion, that it rose higher. French intelligence sources estimated that the strength of the ALN in April 1956 was about 8,500 fighters and over 21,000 auxiliaries. It should also be noted that the French assessment of ALN killed in action (from 1st November 1954 until 31st March 1956) was 4,885.

In the early months of the insurrection arms for the ALN were extremely scarce, being merely what could be seized from French troops in ambushes, stolen, obtained by bribes or smuggled in. This largely accounted for the lull in guerilla

D   49

fighting during the first part of 1955, and it was not until after Nasser made an arms agreement with Czechoslovakia in September 1955 that arms began to flow a trifle more freely from Egypt into Algeria. It was the late summer of that year before the ALN was really able to arm its 'regulars' with modern weapons, and also to expand its regular fighting strength. Cairo became an assembly point for munitions for the ALN, and military equipment that was smuggled into Algeria came mainly from Czechoslovakia, Yugoslavia and Western Germany.

Nasser gave full vocal support to the Algerian Insurrection, and Cairo Radio, 'Voice of the Arabs', had on 1st November (1954) announced that the insurrection had been launched in Algeria for Algerian Freedom against French Imperialism.

Right from the very beginning French counter measures were limited partly owing to the lack of troops and partly because the French Government could not bring itself to appreciate the seriousness and severity of the insurrection. In general, France was much preoccupied with insurgent troubles in both Tunisia and Morocco, and so had little attention to spare for the explosive situation in Algeria. Although it could be clearly seen that the insurrection was swelling to large proportions, there were hesitation and delay in formally recognizing it for what it actually was.

Acting on the assumption that external agitators were trying to stir up tribal revolts in the Constantine, Aures and Kabylie regions, the army moved in to crush them in the traditional manner.[1] At the end of November 1954, and on into December, French aircraft and ground troops combined to comb the mountains to flush out the 'rebels'. The French Army concentrated in particular on the Aures Mountains (Wilaya I) where most of the incidents had occurred so far. Except for the spasmodic bomb-throwing in cities and towns and isolated ambushes in the mountains and countryside, there was little real guerilla activity and so the French military commanders might

[1] In one of the first actions, on 29th November 1954, two French paratroop companies killed 29 insurgents and captured 18, for the loss of 2 men.

be excused for arriving at this deduction. French military operations in the Aures Mountains had a greater degree of success than was apparent, and they caused Ben Boulaid's insurgents to scramble frantically into the mountain vastnesses to avoid annihilation. This pattern was repeated in both the north Constantine (Wilaya II) and the Kabylie (Wilaya III) regions.

For several months after this, French counter-insurgency operations consisted mainly of manning posts in insurgent territory, sending out strong patrols, setting ambushes and instigating large-scale 'cordon-and-search' tactics. The posts, usually strong stone-built blockhouses, situated along routes, in valleys and near mountain passes, had the disadvantage that they only controlled the limited area around them that could be covered by their guns, so ALN detachments could bypass them. Also, the comings and goings of the small French garrisons were watched closely by the ALN auxiliaries, who quickly reported to the insurgent detachments, which were sometimes able to ambush the reliefs.

French commando-type fighting patrols caused alarm and uneasiness amongst the insurgents, but there were not enough of them, owing to the comparatively small number of French troops in Algeria. Even with units returning fairly fast from Indo-China, by May 1955 there were barely 100,000 soldiers in Algeria. Another drawback was that patrols stayed only momentarily in villages and so could not give complete 24-hour protection from the ALN to the villagers. Consequently, villagers were afraid to pass on information about the insurgents lest there be reprisals when the French patrol moved on.

As a general rule the French ambushes were not a great success, although they netted a number of insurgents and auxiliaries, mainly because the auxiliaries quickly spotted the positions and passed on the information to the nearest insurgent detachments, enabling them to take avoiding action. Whenever enough troops could be mustered the French organized large-scale sweeps and 'cordon-and-search' operations. These severely disrupted and frightened the not-too-well-organized or confident ALN groups, but invariably they failed to capture or kill many ALN personnel because the cordon was seldom completed in time, the auxiliaries usually detecting and reporting the movement at an early stage.

French military operations were conventional ones, based to some extent on small, mobile columns, although some anti-insurgent tactics and methods learnt in Indo-China were tentatively employed. The early successes of the insurgents, such as they were, and the fact they were able to survive the guerilla period, must be put down to shortage of French troops, who were insufficient in number to both protect the cities and towns and to go out into the mountains and countryside to hunt out and track down insurgents.

Another drawback was that the French troops were restricted in many ways because there was delay in declaring a state of emergency and granting them adequate powers to conduct the war against the insurgents on more equal terms. The National Assembly did not declare a State of Emergency in Algeria until 31st March 1955, and then at first it was left to the discretion of the Governor-General as to where it should be applied. It was only initially operative in the areas of Batna, Tizi Ouzou, Tebessa and the Kabylie Mountain region, and later along parts of the country adjacent to the Tunisian border. It was not until 30th August 1955 that the State of Emergency was applied to the whole of Algeria, when the prefects, the administrative heads of departments, were allowed to control movement of people within their areas, to create security zones with special rules, and to remove sections of the population. Also, police and army powers of search and arrest were very much widened.

The need for more French troops in Algeria was obvious, but only with reluctance were they provided by the Government — and slowly. In August 1955, the draft of the previous year had its period of service extended and the recall of reservists was authorized, but this was hardly the complete answer. For some time there was, perhaps under American and other Western pressures, a reluctance to weaken the NATO shield in Europe, but as the requirement in Algeria became more desperate, two French divisions were withdrawn from Germany and sent to the eastern part of Algeria. Also, other French units were brought into the country from France, Germany and French West Africa, until the total number topped the 250,000 mark. In April (1956) it was decreed that French conscripts be used in Algeria, and that up to 200,000 reservists be recalled for the same purpose. The plan was that there should be about 400,000 French soldiers in Algeria by the autumn (1956), which number it was estimated would be sufficient to cope with and crush the insurrection fairly quickly.

Territorial Units were raised, manned by Europeans who were liable for so many days' service a year, with the object of taking over many static defence tasks in cities and towns, enabling regular troops to be released for operations in the field.

Apart from military measures to crush the insurrection, the French Government, still believing that social and economic causes were the root of the Algerian Muslim discontent, instigated agrarian reforms, set up medical centres in the villages and propagated the spread of education by building hundreds of classrooms and staffing them with soldiers, as there was a shortage of teachers. Also, construction and other rehabilitation projects were begun. Psychological warfare, on the pattern learnt in Indo-China, was tentatively and cautiously played with by the army. Officers and non-commissioned officers were seconded to the civil administration to go out to look after and live in the remotest villages, many of which had been neglected by the Government for so long. It seemed as though with one hand the army was trying to crush the insurrection by force, while with the other it was trying to kill the insurgents and the people with kindness and consideration.

Concurrent with the expansion of the Wilayas in the country-side was an attempt to organize an ALN underground movement in the cities which had the dual purpose of dominating the Muslim population and terrorizing the Europeans. At first the terror tactics were aimed at known pro-French Muslims and those appointed to official positions. The victims were first warned by letter to cease co-operating with the French Government, and then if they ignored the warning, they were assassinated. This action impressed and frightened the Muslims, showing that the ALN was a ruthless and capable organization that meant what it said. These assassinations were undertaken by the 'military arm' of the ALN underground, which was made up of small cells on the Communist pattern, each with either a political or military role.

In Algiers, for example, killing of important personalities was the task of the political cells, which produced specially trained executioners for a particular job. They would fire at the victim with a revolver or pistol, and then disappear quickly into the crowd. The ALN political branch became very expert at organizing such assassinations.

The military cells of the ALN underground were used for indiscriminate terrorism in the cities, when the usual method was to throw bombs into European crowds. This caused fear and uneasiness, which in turn resulted in tying down more troops on security duties in the cities, and so leaving fewer available to hunt insurgents in the mountains and countryside. The authorities had to use repressive measures, which made them more unpopular with the Muslim masses. This practice of indiscriminate bomb-throwing caused friction to increase between the two communities, Muslim and the European.

Even before launching the insurrection, CRUA had a fairly strong and well-organized underground movement in Algiers, and control of this was gained by Belkacem Krim, when he moved his headquarters into that city. In the early days of the insurrection the ALN underground was extremely short of both bombs and explosives, and also the technical knowledge to produce home-made ones. This forced it, more or less unwillingly, to co-operate with the Communists, who were more expert at this sort of thing, and who even had a secret 'backstreet' arsenal.

The PCA, which had in haste openly condemned the insurrection in the first place, was soon sitting back biting its nails in chagrin, as it watched the ALN, despite setbacks, grow in

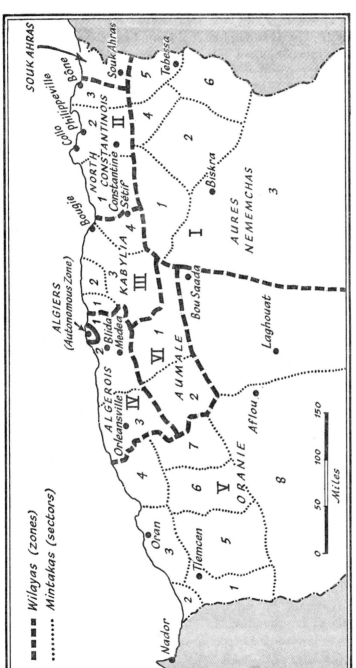

Algeria, showing Wilayas

Wilayas (zones)
Mintakas (sectors)

SOUKAHRAS

Bône
Collo
Philippeville
Bougie
Souk Ahras
Tebessa

NORTH
CONSTANTINOIS
Constantine
Sétif

II

KABYLIA

III

AURES
NEMEMCHAS

I

Biskra

Laghouat

Bou Saada

AUMALE

VI

Blida
Medea

ALGIERS
(Autonomous Zone)

ALGÉROIS
Orléansville

IV

Aflou

ORANIE

V

Oran
Tlemcen

Nador

Miles

0   50   100   150

50   100   150

strength. The Communists could not bear the thought of a national revolution of this nature happening without their active support, so they agreed to give unofficial aid by providing explosives and showing ALN terrorists how to make home-made bombs. In this way, both explosives and technical knowledge were gained, enabling ALN personnel to steal, or otherwise obtain, the essential ingredients.

After some hesitation, the PCA came out openly on the side of the insurgents, which caused the Government, in September 1955, to dissolve the Party and ban its two newspapers.[1] This drove the PCA leadership and active members underground. The Chairman of the PCA Central Committee was Saddock Hajeres, a Jew, appointed by Moscow persuasion as probably being more acceptable in any dispute between Muslims and Christians. Apart from minor co-operation on manufacturing and obtaining explosives, the two underground organizations in Algiers, the PCA and the ALN, had little to do with each other, each contenting itself with warily and stonily eyeing the other for several months. The PCA formed a small para-military organization in the city. The PCA probably had about 12,000 members, of whom about 80 per cent were European, many of Spanish descent who sympathized with the Spanish Republicans. As the war progressed there was a change of heart on the part of the European Communists, who turned against the Muslims, dropping their political activities and affiliations. Soon most were loudly shouting for a French Algeria.

The underground struggle for control of the Muslim population of Algiers continued, with another contender taking the field. In 1955, Messali Hadj had formed the members of the officially dissolved MTLD (banned on suspicion of involvement in the insurrection) into the 'Mouvement National Algérien' (Algerian National Movement), the MNA, and with it he set about gaining control over the Muslims in Algiers. The MNA quickly became powerful, spreading outside Algiers and rivalling the underground ALN.

Seeing how the insurrection was going, Messali Hadj wanted

[1] *Liberté* and '*Alger Républicain*'.

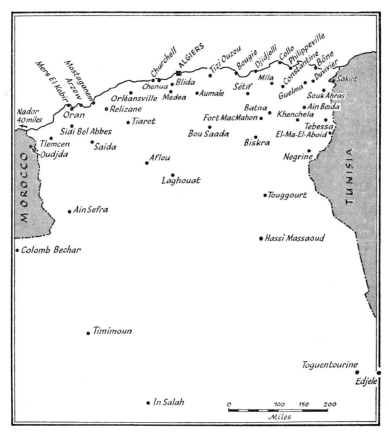

Algeria, showing some place names

to join with the FLN, but on his own terms, and he ordered his MNA representative in Cairo to negotiate with Ben Bella for MNA entry *en bloc* into the FLN. Ben Bella would not agree, insisting that the MNA must first disband, when its members, if they rejected their old allegiances, could individually join the FLN. Although Messali Hadj agreed in principle, he hesitated to implement his decision, and began intriguing with other Algerian nationalist politicians. When Ben Bella discovered that Messali Hadj was trying to persuade Ulema and UDMA members to gang up against him, he persuaded the Egyptian authorities to arrest MNA agents in Cairo, thus causing open hostility to break out between the FLN and the MNA.

In Algiers there was fighting between the two groups, as Belkacem Krim, assisted by Ramdane Abbane, mounted an underground offensive against Messali Hadj's men. As many MNA members put on ALN uniforms for convenience to carry out insurgent activities, this internecine struggle accounted for the many dead bodies wearing ALN uniforms that were found by the French during 1955, especially as the struggle spread to the mountains and countryside. Apart from being well organized, strong and active in Algiers, already in March (1955) the MNA had started to operate in the Orléansville sector, and the following month MNA units appeared in Kabylie, where there was fighting between them and the ALN. Generally, but not always, the ALN was slightly more successful, and gradually MNA armed groups were pushed southwards. In fighting this rival revolutionary organization, the ALN suffered many casualties it could ill afford.

The struggle between the FLN and the MNA spread to France, where it took bitter shape in Paris amongst the resident Muslim population. Both organizations demanded money for their funds, which was obtained by threats and terrorism. Many innocent Algerian Muslims in France were killed, and also sometimes tortured by one group on suspicion of helping the other.

In April 1956, Saddock Hajeres of the PCA met Ramdane Abbane in Algiers, proposing that the PCA should enter the FLN *en bloc*. Ramdane Abbane, who was negotiating for the

FLN, would not agree, insisting that the PCA must disband completely first, when its members could join the ALN provided they forswore their former allegiances. Saddock Hajeres would not accept this condition, which virtually drove him into the arms of the MNA. There was some co-operation between the PCA and the MNA, especially in the Orléansville area, but in fact this never amounted to very much.

Following further meetings between Saddock Hajeres and Ramdane Abbane, the PCA agreed to limited co-operation with the ALN in Algiers, when a small number of 'Maquis Rouge', or 'Liberation Fighters' were placed under ALN command. In addition about 100 Algerian Muslim Communists individually joined the ALN. The secret 'back-street' arsenal also passed to the ALN.

As soon as they were with the ALN, the Communists, in the usual Communist manner, attempted to mix politics with fighting and to loudly preach their own political creed at every opportunity. They sought to penetrate the organization and to subvert it to their own purposes. Both Belkacem Krim and Ramdane Abbane saw what was happening, and the Maquis Rouge squads, of which there were about half a dozen, were ruthlessly and callously committed into action against the French Army and police until they were practically eliminated, as were many of the other Communists with the ALN. Next, using a Communist gambit, Ramdane Abbane accused the PCA Central Committee of treachery, and in Algiers the full weight of the underground ALN was turned against the Communists, who were either eliminated or driven into hiding. The shrewd Ramdane Abbane (who was assisted in this task by Ben Khedda, who had moved into Algiers) had recognized and promptly dealt with a classic Communist tactic. After this the Communists played almost no part of any importance in the whole course of the insurrection.

Determined to deprive the French of the support of the Algerian Muslim politicians, ALN terrorist pressure was brought to bear against Muslims elected to the Algerian Assembly, who became known as the '61 Group' because of their number. This

59

group published a statement in September 1955,[1] condemning integration[2] with France and French repressive measures against the insurgents, and on 1st January 1956 all the members of the '61 Group' resigned in a body. An impasse was only avoided by indefinite postponement of elections for the Algerian Assembly. In April (1956), the Algerian Assembly was dissolved and its powers were assumed by the Governor-General.

Meanwhile, many prominent Muslim politicians, seeing which way the wind was blowing, went underground, either joining the ALN in Algiers or making their way to Cairo to join the FLN External Delegation. Threats by the ALN persuaded many to take either one or the other of these courses. In January 1956, Tewfik El Madani, a Ulema leader, declared in favour of the FLN, but one of the best catches of the year was Ferhat Abbas, who had, when leading the UDMA, initially condemned the insurrection. After working underground with the ALN in Algiers for a whort while he arrived openly in Cairo in April (1956) to join the FLN. It was alleged that Ferhat Abbas had been frightened into taking this step. His nephew had been assassinated, after the customary warning, for co-operating with the French authorities. Immediately, the killer was shot down by the police, and it was said that in the assassin's pocket was an ALN document ordering the assassination of Ferhat Abbas himself.

Nationalists in North Africa decided to hold public demonstrations on the second anniversary of the exile of the Sultan of Morocco (20th August 1955), to symbolize the solidarity of the North African peoples. The FLN agreed to co-operate and set about organizing them in Algeria. Under FLN instructions some demonstrations occurred in Algiers and other major cities in the country, but all were less than half-hearted and a great disappointment to the FLN. They indicated clearly that the FLN did not yet have either the support of, or control over, the Muslim masses.

In Wilaya II (the north Constantine region) the insurgents

[1] Manifeste des 61.
[2] The word 'integration' had come to replace that of 'assimilation'.

chose this day to launch a series of attacks, in which over 100 French and Europeans died and many were wounded, as a reprisal for the alleged killing of Muslim civilians by the French. French troops quickly moved into the area and took punitive action that caused the insurgents heavy losses. More insurgent and Muslim casualties occurred in the subsequent waves of individual European reprisals.

Based on Cairo, the External Delegation of the FLN was having more success, especially in the diplomatic field, attracting considerable notice overseas to its cause. Perhaps its first major diplomatic achievement was persuading Arab and other 'friendly' countries to cause the UN General Assembly to consider the Algerian problem on 30th September 1955. Asserting that this was purely a domestic matter, France as a protest walked out of the debate. Another important diplomatic step to internationalize their struggle was when a FLN delegation, consisting of Hocine Ait Ahmed and Mohammed Yazid, attended the Bandung Conference, where they lobbied the cause to sympathetic listeners. The declared FLN aim was to establish a sovereign state in Algeria, headed by popular leaders who could make decisions independent from French influence. At this juncture the FLN did not go so far as to demand complete independence on a republican pattern.

A public demonstration was called for by the FLN in Algiers to celebrate the victory at the UN on 30th September, but this proved to be very disappointing. The trade unions would not co-operate,[1] and none of the three major ones were at all nationalistically inclined. Attempts were made to coerce them, but without much success.

In February 1956, Messali Hadj formed his own trade union, the 'Union Syndicale des Travailleurs Algériens' (the Syndicate Union of Algerian Workers), the USTA, through which he hoped to obtain a grip on the Muslim workers in Algiers, as

---

[1] The three main trade unions in Algeria were the Communist-controlled Confédération Générale du Travail, the CGT; the Socialist-controlled Force Ouvrière, the FO; and the Catholic-controlled Confédération Française de Travailleurs, the CFTC.

well as other main cities and towns of Algeria, and also the Muslim workers in France.

As a riposte, in March, Ben Khedda formed a FLN trade union, the 'Union Générale des Travailleurs Algériens' (the General Union of Algerian Workers), the UGTA. The two rival unions then fought for recruits and influence. As a rough guide, during the following months the FLN-sponsored UGTA had more success in Algeria, while Messali Hadj's USTA did better in France. There were frequent clashes between members of the rival unions. By May, the UGTA claimed to have some 110,000 members but in that month its Secretary-General, Aissat Idir, was arrested, and it was forced to move its headquarters to Tunis.

The first stage of the insurrection was entirely military in character, and had no support from the Muslim masses other than what it obtained at pistol-point. For the first 14 months, the ALN leaders seemed to care little about putting their ideology over to the Muslim people and to enlist their willing help. Terrorism seemed to produce the required results, and universal Muslim dislike for French rule was taken for granted. The comparative failure of the 20th August and 30th September demonstrations brought home to the FLN that the Muslim masses were still largely indifferent, not to say hostile, to its cause. More pressure was put on Muslim politicians, who wavered amongst themselves, and one by one they came out in support of the FLN. By December 1955, it was more apparent that the ALN was a force to reckon with in Algeria, if for no other reason than to escape assassination for alleged collaboration with the French authorities.

By this time the ALN had completed the survival stage of the insurgent war. Guerilla groups had become well established in the mountains of the northern part of Algeria, and so it was decided to turn attention to winning the Muslim population completely over to its cause.

This campaign, for the minds of the Muslim people, began in December 1955, and lasted for about three months, during which the revolutionary ideals and aims of the FLN were fully explained. The plan was that there would first have to be terror combined with a little persuasion and re-education, and that the terror element would gradually be eased off. In this period FLN agents went amongst the people preaching, persuading and threatening, sowing the seeds of revolt in all minds. Calculated terror was employed initially; in particular French-appointed Caids, or village headmen, school teachers and officials were killed to remove their restraining and reasoning influence from the people. This intensive FLN propaganda campaign was so successful that by February (1956) the bulk of the Muslim population had become pro-FLN, anxious and willing to help the ALN in its insurgent activities, without the pressure of terror or threats, or the fear of reprisals if they did not do so.

Thus the FLN and the ALN had accomplished two major insurgent requirements, the armed forces had survived and the willing support of the people had been gained. Both were major advantages. Until December 1955, it would have been possible for the French to have driven a wedge between the Muslim masses and the FLN organization which, if followed by prompt and wise political reforms, might have knocked the whole FLN platform down and caused the motivation of the revolt to shrivel.

With the bulk of the Muslim people on its side, with more arms coming from Egypt, with more recruits coming forward and a new enthusiasm for the insurrection sweeping through the country, in March 1956 the ALN decided to embark upon greater offensive action against the French forces. The morale of the ALN was rising after a period of depression. The ALN leaders reckoned they were entering the protracted stage of insurgent warfare.

The Wilayas first set about enlarging their firm bases and extending the terrain they dominated. Larger sections of the population were brought under control, and as it gained a firmer grip, the ALN governed with a firmer hand. Taxes were levied and justice meted out. The people were protected from raids and depredations from other tribes and bandits, and feuds were settled. As soon as medical supplies were available, the ALN started village clinics, primarily for their own use, but they were also made available to the villagers. Later, the ALN set up schools for the children. Men were conscripted into either the regular or auxiliary element of the ALN. There was now less opposition to this forcible recruiting than formerly, when at times replacements for ALN battle casualties had to be taken by press-gang methods, and the recruits so obtained were only kept fighting in the ALN ranks by threats of reprisals to the man's family. More willing and enthusiastic co-operation of the Muslim masses enabled the ALN to enlarge and improve its intelligence service, and thus another vitally important advantage was gained.

By March 1956, the ALN had obtained control over large sections of the Aures and Nementcha Mountains, Kabylie and the Constantine area. The small town of Collo, on the Collo Peninsula, for example, had been virtually besieged since September 1955, and had to be supplied by sea. Part of the frontier region near the Tunisian border passed completely under insurgent domination, as did a section of terrain adjacent to the Moroccan frontier over to the west, where Tlemcen was still partially besieged. The ALN was slowly spreading out in the countryside from its firm bases, according to plan.

Beginning in February (1956) the French Army worked out a new strategy of pacification. So far it had operated as it had always done when faced with tribal uprisings, by relying basically on mobile punitive columns. The new tactics became known as the 'quadrillage' system, or grid system, under which all the major cities and towns were garrisoned in strength, and other towns, villages and farms were similarly garrisoned in diminishing strength. This tied up vast numbers of troops, leaving comparatively few for mobile operations, but had the advantage that it sat heavily on the main centres of population and communications. The quadrillage system entailed full co-operation between the military, the police and the civilian administration at all levels, the accent usually being on the force mostly involved, such as the police in the cities, and the army in the rural areas, but each helped the other additionally whenever possible. Linked to this was the civil development programme, which consisted of building roads, clinics and schools, which got under way as the army smothered guerilla activity.

Mustering what shock troops it could without denuding the garrisons under the quadrillage system, a French counteroffensive was mounted during April and May and had considerable success, the ALN having to give ground and fall back to avoid incurring heavy casualties. With good intelligence and air support, the ground troops were able to search out and harry the insurgents. Weight of modern fire power told against the ALN fighters, who were soon short of ammunition, and hardly adequately trained to stand up to French soldiers in a pitched battle. The ALN policy was to operate in as large units as possible, guerilla tactics being pushed into the background in the eagerness to hit and smash units of the French forces. These tactics were disastrous, and during these two months over 6,000 insurgents were killed in action, out of a probable total of 18,000 armed men.[1] The ALN spring offensive, which had started with such high hopes, had to be called off.

Next, the French marked out insurgent areas, such as the Collo Peninsula, parts of the Aures Mountains, Kabylie and Oran Province. These were heavily patrolled, and the population where possible moved into specially built camps near military garrisons for protection.

The French employed about 180,000 'harkis', Algerian Muslim auxiliary fighters, many of whom were mounted on horses, and these became a special target for FLN agents. ALN subversive efforts had caused a steady outflow of Muslim deserters, often with their arms. Also, assistance was sometimes given to the insurgents by the Muslim soldiers in the French forces; for example in February 1956 a small unit of harkis, in an engagement with the ALN near the Moroccan frontier, had changed sides during the battle. There were other similar, but lesser, incidents. In August, a Muslim lieutenant was imprisoned for

---

[1] Official French sources state that 13,899 insurgents were killed in action between 1st April and 31st December 1956.

passing military information to the FLN. To try and remove this weakness, during the summer (of 1956) several French Muslim units in Algeria were transferred to Germany or France and replaced by French ones.

Unhappy, unstable French domestic politics did not help solve the Algerian problem. French Governments, never very firmly installed, were subject to so many conflicting pressure groups. There was a vocal Communist influence in France that was very much against harsh measures being taken in Algeria, while on the other hand the powerful Europeans, becoming angry over the constant incidents of terrorism, wanted firmer action to be taken. There was resistance in France to the recall of so many reservists to serve in Algeria, which was expressed in incidents of disobedience and reluctance. Sending conscripts to serve in that country was not popular in many quarters either.

In January 1955, Jacques Soustelle was appointed Governor-General of Algeria, and he made some administrative changes, drawing officers from the army, for example, to look after areas that had previously been neglected or under-administered. This caused some friction between the army and the civil administration, the latter having European sympathies to a large extent. Soustelle was extremely unpopular with the Europeans in Algeria, who were not prepared to surrender any of their privileges, and they did what they could to nullify his measures.

The general election in France in January 1956 enabled Guy Mollet to form a left-wing coalition government. Mollet decided to appoint General Catroux[1] Governor-General of Algeria in place of Soustelle, and he went to Algiers personally to install him. General Catroux had just negotiated with the exiled Sultan of Morocco for the withdrawal of French troops from Morocco—a bad omen from the Europeans' point of view, who suspected he would begin negotiations with the FLN leaders. Mollet's reception in Algiers by the Europeans was so abusive and violent that he cancelled General Catroux's appointment. A short-lived Committee of Public Safety was formed, which

---

[1] General Catroux had been briefly Governor-General of Algeria during World War II.

lasted a few days until Robert Lacoste, who was acceptable to the Europeans, was appointed in his stead on 10th February. Lacoste had the title of Resident Minister for Algeria. This demonstrated the Europeans' influence and gave them confidence that violent agitation would get them their own way, but its impact caused Mollet to work for a cease-fire in Algeria.

Morocco and Tunisia were granted independence by France in March 1956, and both new governments sympathized actively with the FLN. The External Delegation of the FLN opened offices in Rabat and Tunis, and with the assistance of Moroccans and Tunisians began to organize better arms and supply routes into Algeria. Also, Moroccan and Tunisian territory could now be used as a secure, unhindered refuge for the ALN. Previously, the presence of French troops had been a bar to this.

In the same month, the Arab League denounced French use of NATO troops against the ALN, and pledged support and aid. On 28th July, Nasser nationalized the Suez Canal, thus focusing world attention momentarily on Egypt.

Inside Algeria, the summer of 1956 was not a particularly good one for the ALN. Crude and conventional as they were, French military operations had done much to hinder, upset and disorganize the insurgent forces, whose casualty rate caused morale to slide steadily downwards. Although guerilla groups were firmly established in all five Wilayas, they all had a recruiting problem. It was true that the bulk of the Muslim masses were now in full sympathy with FLN ideals, but it was a passive sympathy, and the people had yet to be prodded into activity in this cause. Despite the example of the achievements of neighbouring Morocco and Tunisia, the spirit of the revolution was not such that volunteer fighters came tumbling in, and so compulsory methods had to be continued.

The ALN had hardly recovered from the severe jolt given by the French forces in the spring. Machinery was being put in motion to call up more French conscripts. This indicated that determined efforts were about to be made to crush the insurgents, who would then be in grave danger of annihilation. In addition, the armed groups of the hostile MNA remained a worry, and so were — to a lesser extent — the still fairly numerous unreliable tribal chiefs and bandit groups in the mountains, who cared little or nothing for revolutionary ideals.

There was uneasiness, discontent and friction between the various Wilaya commanders, who tended to be a trifle jealous of each other's achievements. Belkacem Krim, who had moved out of his Wilaya (in Kabylie) to join Amar Ouamrane and Ramdane Abbane in Algiers, where he was becoming dominant, was suspected of intriguing for the leadership of the ALN in Algeria. All Wilaya commanders complained bitterly of lack of interest on the part of the External Delegation, lack of guidance and firm instructions and lack of arms and supplies. Communications between Algeria and Cairo were poor, and thus tended to make field commanders suspicious of Ben Bella and other members of the External Delegation, who were getting the limelight and building up personal prestige without personal danger, to the neglect of the vital needs of the ALN fighting desperately for its existence in Algeria. That these complaints were general and continuing could be seen in the pages of *El Mouadjahed*, the official periodical of the FLN, issued monthly in Arabic and French, and edited for a time by Ben Khedda, which openly discussed them.

In the cities there was depression as an efficient police force continually arrested FLN agents and key underground ALN personnel, thus hamstringing activities. The rival underground MNA remained a dangerous enemy too.

At the close of the first phase of the insurrection, after the first twenty months, neither side quite realized what the true position was. The French had the opportunity of stepping quickly in to crush a bewildered, slightly embittered guerilla army that was spread out in five, uneven, unco-ordinated sections, and not in a position to offer much serious opposition. The ALN hold on the minds of the Muslim people was not yet sufficient for it to be completely safe for the insurgents to merge as of routine into the general population when hard pressed. The French intelligence service was too efficient and capable.

But the French authorities hesitated. They noted the Moroccan and Tunisian examples and to them it appeared that about one-third of northern Algeria was insurgent-affected. Daily there were ambushes, guerilla attacks and bomb-throwing incidents. Cautiously, it was decided to wait until the autumn, by which time more reinforcements would have arrived, before launching the first part of an offensive they hoped would be completely successful by the spring of 1957.

On the other hand, despite sinking morale and shortages, the ALN was having more success in winning the minds of the people than was apparent. More arms and supplies were on the way, and the full benefit of the use of Moroccan and Tunisian territory was yet to be felt and appreciated by the ALN.

CHAPTER 4

The Second Phase
(August 1956 – May 1958)

The second phase of the Algerian Insurrection lasted from August 1956, when the Soummam Conference was held, until the spring of 1958, when General de Gaulle returned to power, and it covers a period of confused French governmental policy and weak handling of the Algerian problem.

Lack of early anticipated success in the field, coupled with the uneasy state of the ALN and the absence of clear-cut guiding principles and policy, resulted in a meeting of leaders which became known as the Soummam Conference. This was because it met in the Soummam Valley, in Kabylie, on 20th August 1956, a gesture attributed to the External Delegation as being designed to placate the field commanders of the ALN. But the External Delegation never arrived. Led by Ben Bella, it waited impatiently in Italy for about three weeks for the signal to slip secretly into Algeria. But this signal never came. Instead, the External Delegation was warned that the French police had become aware of its projected move and intention. Eventually, it crossed over into Tripoli, only to learn that the Soummam Conference had taken place without it. Ben Bella had not been able to dominate, guide and lead the FLN and ALN personnel as he had wanted, or to impose on them his policy and ideas; on the contrary, he was presented with what the Conference had decided in his absence as a *fait accompli*.

This serious mismanagement was most probably primarily due to poor communication and bad liaison between the External Delegation in Cairo and the Internal Delegation inside

Algeria. But another, more sinister, interpretation has been placed on the incident, which was that the External Delegation was deliberately kept in ignorance of the time and place of the Soummam Conference by Ramdane Abbane, its organizer. As Ramdane Abbane was an ambitious man with a mind of his own, who tended at times to disagree with Ben Bella, this may contain some element of truth, and certain aspects raise suspicions.

In all, just over 200 delegates from the ALN in Algeria attended this Conference, at which the leading personalities were: Belkacem Krim, of Wilaya III; Amar Ouamrane, representing Wilaya IV, although he had not been formally appointed to command; and Ramdane Abbane, the political liaison officer. A notable absentee was Omar Ben Boulaid, of Wilaya I, which was still in a rather unsettled state, although he did send a representative. Domination by these personalities at the Conference has been seen by some as an effort to make the Berbers the leading figures in the revolution, but this is a far more doubtful supposition. It is true that the French began to exploit the feuds and differences among the Berber tribes, and between the Berbers and the Arabs, but without a great deal of success. Although Ramdane Abbane and his senior colleagues pushed their own ideas forward, they all wanted to forge a working revolutionary organization, and an army that would be able to fight, and were not keen on any particular section, tribe or faction, becoming too much in the majority or the ascendancy.

A document containing proposals and suggestions, allegedly written by Ramdane Abbane in advance in liaison with the External Delegation, was produced at the Conference and most of its resolutions were, after discussion, adopted. It affirmed collective leadership, and internal matters were to take priority over external ones. Measures were to be taken to narrow down external and internal differences. Political and military relationships were defined, with politics always taking precedence and a Socialist political programme was adopted.

The Conference set up the 'Conseil National de la Révolution Algérienne' (the National Council of the Algerian Revolution), the CNRA, a sort of central committee or governing body, which was composed of 17 members. Also, 17 substitutes were named to cater for casualties, making a total of 34 people. Members and substitutes were selected from both the External and Internal Delegations. In fact, some names were only a matter of form, such as that of Mustapha Ben Boulaid, named a member, who had been killed some five months previously, and Aissat Idir, the Secretary-General of the UGTA, who was in prison, where he died.

The security arrangements for the Soummam Conference were good and the French authorities were not aware of its existence at the time, nor were they in fact until its findings were made public on 1st November 1956, the third anniversary of the insurrection, when lists of members and substitutes of the CNRA were published in full. Several of the personalities were unknown to the police, and others were thought to have been killed. If this could have been done so well, it does seem remarkable that the organizer, the efficient Ramdane Abbane, was not able to smuggle into Algeria at least some members of the External Delegation. But there is always in young revolutionary movements jealousy and intrigue in the struggle for leadership and status.

The Soummam Conference created the 'Comité de Coordination et d'Exécution' (Committee of Co-ordination and Execution), the CCE, an executive body consisting in the first instance of five members: Belkacem Krim, Ramdane Abbane, Ben Khedda and Aissat Idir. As the latter was in prison, it was thought that his name was included as a sop to certain trade union and civilian elements of the FLN. The names of members of the CCE were not made public.

It was agreed to launch a terrorist offensive in Algeria.

The Conference also laid down details for the standardization of the ALN. Ranks were introduced, and each of the Wilaya commanders became a colonel, it being decided that no generals would be appointed in the ALN until after the 'liberation'. Each colonel had three majors to assist him, who were responsible respectively for political affairs, military operations and liaison-intelligence. The colonel was as much a military governor as a field commander, and he had an elected consultative assembly, usually of about five people, to both advise on and deal with civil, financial, economic and Islamic problems. Each Wilaya had its own taxation organization and courts of justice. Separate propaganda sections were formed, specializing in psychological warfare. All officer promotions and demotions had to be approved by the CCE, but Wilaya commanders retained the freedom to make junior promotions below officer level.

The task of the CCE was to ensure smooth working and liaison between the Wilayas, and to ensure that all followed the master plans decided upon. Previously each Wilaya had been very much a law unto itself, and there were jealousy and suspicion between Wilaya commanders. This had shown itself in the distribution of illicit arms obtained by the External Delegation, when the Wilayas near the borders of Tunisia and Morocco held on to all they could get. It was alleged that even 18 months after the outbreak of the insurrection Wilaya III (Kabylie) had no automatic weapons at all, as Wilayas I and II would not allow any to pass through their territory, but seized all for their own use.

The Wilayas were divided into zones (mintaka),[1] each commanded by a captain, who was assisted by three lieutenants, each responsible for one of the staff sections. The zones were further divided into regions (nahia), under a second-lieutenant, assisted by three cadets. In turn the regions were made up of sections, the smallest territorial subdivision, each commanded by a warrant officer.

Previously units had been too large and unwieldy, and of uneven composition. This was regularized by laying down that the basic field unit was to be the battalion, which was to have

[1]
Wilaya I	had 6 zones	Wilaya IV	had 3 zones
Wilaya II	had 3 zones	Wilaya V	had 9 zones
Wilaya III	had 3 zones	Wilaya VI	had 2 zones.

three companies, with a total strength of 20 officers and 350 men. Each company was to have three platoons, and a strength of five officers and 110 men. The platoon was to consist of three groups. Mostly, especially during the following months, the battalion commander was also the zone commander, and indeed most of the officers doubled up by holding an appointment in a battalion and also carrying out an additional administrative role. As more arms were received and more men recruited, independent battalions appeared in which the officers and men concentrated solely upon training, tactics and fighting. At all levels, from the Wilaya right down to the section, and from the battalion right down to the platoon, the collective principle of command was applied, with the political officer participating in all decisions and being consulted in all matters. It took between six and eight months to obtain uniformity on these lines in all the Wilayas, after which there was a gradual spread of good discipline and better training.

The blue-print for insurgent warfare as expounded by Mao Tse-tung, and as practised by General Giap in Indo-China, had been carefully studied, and Muslims were organized into three separate elements in the ALN. The first consisted of the uniformed fighters, the full-time 'regular' soldiers, who were known as 'moujahidines'. These were the spearhead of the insurrection, and the Soummam Conference introduced a pay scale for them, which varied from 1,000 fr. a month for a private soldier up to 5,000 fr. for a colonel. In addition, their families received monthly allowances, those in rural areas being given 2,000 fr. for the wife, and 2,000 fr. for each dependant. In urban districts the allowance for a wife was 5,000 fr. The cash paid out was obtained by blackmail, extortion and terrorism from Muslims in both Algeria and France.

The second element consisted of the para-military auxiliaries, known as 'moussebilines', who had no uniform and functioned on a part-time basis, carrying out their normal occupations for most of the time but being available to give support to the regular element when required. They were given some military training, and later on, as more arms became available, a proportion

74

were armed. They served as guides, sentries, messengers, saboteurs and intelligence agents, and they formed a sort of reserve upon which the regular element could call to help out in an emergency. The moussebilines were unpaid. The other military element consisted of the part-time helpers and fighters in the villages, who were known as the 'fidayines'.

They were less organized and barely trained, but were available on a part-time basis to carry out supporting tasks whenever units of the regular part of the ALN required assistance in their area. They also acted as smugglers, porters, sentries and intelligence agents, as well as occasionally carrying out minor acts of terrorism. Ramdane Abbane had visualized the moussebilines and fidayines increasingly taking on guerilla activity while the regular element was withdrawn to develop into a 'conventional army' ready for the ultimate battle. He did not think the French economy could maintain 400,000 troops in the country indefinitely.

The political and administrative body of the ALN became known as the 'Organisation Politico-Administrative', the OPA, and was made up of the key agents and planners, who used the services of the moussebilines and fidayines.

Women were declared to be equal in the ALN and received the same rates of pay, but the numbers serving were extremely small. Mainly they were employed as nurses, in administrative jobs and, if their standard of education was high enough, as teachers or clerks, or in the political branch.

The next momentous event occurred on 22nd October 1956, when Ben Bella and other FLN leaders were virtually kidnapped when on board a Moroccan aircraft. Relations between the FLN and the Sultan of Morocco were not too good, and Ben Bella had visited him for talks to see if they could be improved, and more Moroccan aid given to the ALN and more Moroccan support lent to the FLN in the diplomatic field. The aircraft, which had a French crew who were not involved in the plot at all, was 'talked down' when flying over Algeria and the passengers arrested. With Ben Bella were Mohammed Khider, Hocine Ait Ahmed and Mohammed Boudiaf, all prominent in the FLN and members of the original 'Club of Nine'. This left only one member at large, Belkacem Krim: of the others, three were dead and now five were prisoners.

This act caused great indignation and outcry on the part of the Arab states, who regarded it as a gross breach of traditional hospitality and an act of unparalleled treachery. It was a terrific morale booster for the FLN and the ALN, and a powerful propaganda weapon in the diplomatic field. The Sultan of Morocco regarded the kidnapped FLN leaders as his personal guests, as they were aboard one of his aircraft.

The French Government disclaimed all responsibility for this kidnapping and said that no minister had given any authority for it. Lacoste, the Resident Minister, knew nothing about it either, and neither had he been contacted nor consulted beforehand. There was an unconvincing air of denial and confusion over this incident. Much later, at his trial, Colonel Gardes disclosed that he, while serving in the intelligence branch in Algeria, had initiated and planned the kidnapping of the FLN leaders. It was all over and done with before any responsible authority, either political or military, knew what was being carried out. There was some debate as to whether or not to release Ben Bella and his companions, but this came to nothing. They were too valuable a capture, and were flown to Paris to be interned.

Another confusing angle on this incident was the allegation that Mollet, the Prime Minister, had been in secret contact with Ben Bella and that a French Government emissary had been sent to Tunisia, where the aircraft was bound, to meet him there. As that was only weakly denied by the French Government, it was probably true. The plain fact was that the French military intelligence service sprang an independent, surprise coup that was disconcertingly successful. On 25th October it was announced by the FLN that Tewfik El Madani, Secretary-General of the Ulema, who had joined the FLN in April 1956, had been appointed leader of the External Delegation in place of Ben Bella.

Documents found in possession of the kidnapped FLN person-nel included a report on falling morale in the ALN, a directive to have nothing to do with the MNA leaders if they asked for negotiations, plans for attacks on French forces and barracks in eastern Algeria, and on the police headquarters in both Oran and Algiers, as well as a list of the French, European and Muslim agents and contacts the FLN was using. This valuable information enabled many FLN agents to be arrested and certain ALN projects to be thwarted.

Although by mid-1956 the Algerian Insurrection had become to some extent a mass movement, there were still a few minority groups in opposition of dissent. The main one was the MNA, led by the exiled Messali Hadj. In parts of the countryside of Algeria armed bands of the MNA continued to fight the ALN, while in Algiers, Paris and other cities in both Algeria and France, an underground struggle to the death was in progress between the two factions. It was a battle for dominance over the Muslim population, and also for Party funds, which were obtained by extortion. Generally, in Algiers the MNA had the worst of this struggle, due largely to the efforts of Ramdane Abbane, who had turned his ability and energy to subduing the Muslims in that city. In France the opposite was the case, and in Paris, where some 120,000 Algerian Muslims worked, 86 Muslims were killed in 1956 as the direct result of the under-ground struggle, many of them being tortured first.

During the latter part of 1956, the ALN underground in Algiers gradually gained control over the majority of Muslims, mainly by terrorist tactics. Bombing incidents and shootings rose in number, month by month. The power and influence of UGTA, the FLN-controlled trade union, slowly increased, but not as fast as was desired. A series of small, hardly successful, strikes preceded a major one, planned to last for eight days. This was to take place in January (1957) to coincide with the UN debate on Algeria, and while there was some initial re-sponse in Algiers, Oran and Constantine, it soon fizzled out.

Indiscriminate bomb-throwing into crowds caused European casualties, and provoked certain extremist elements to hit back.

European counter-terrorist activity can be said to have begun on 30th June (1956) when a bomb exploded at the headquarters of UGTA in Algiers. This was followed, on 17th July, by another explosion at a Communist newspaper office. Other similar incidents occurred with increasing frequency during the latter part of 1956. Anti-Muslim feeling erupted in anti-Muslim riots in Algiers on 29th December, on the occasion of the funeral of a murdered European mayor, when European mobs shouted 'The Army to Power'.

Two extremist European organizations, the CRF, Committee of the Re-birth of France, and the ORAF, the Resistance Organization of French Algeria, conducted violent propaganda campaigns against French Government policy, and also indulged in terrorist activities against Muslims and liberal, or left-wing Europeans. Both were dissolved by Lacoste in December, but continued their activities underground. Already, in the previous July, Lacoste had dissolved the 'French North African Union', a European extremist political group, for activities 'tending to turn the Army against the civil authority'.

European political activities were encouraged by Soustelle from Paris, where French Governments seemed progressively less able to control events in Algeria. The French Governments had always contained an element that wanted to negotiate with the FLN, and this caused anger and anxiety on the part of the Europeans, and even gave indirect stimulus to unlawful violence. Soustelle, who when Governor-General of Algeria had been rather out of sympathy with European views and interests, had changed his views and became their champion.

During 1956, the French quadrillage strategy lay heavily on the country like a wet blanket, keeping ALN units from the centres of population and making insurgency infiltration difficult. Although this strategy left comparatively few troops for a mobile offensive role, the French Army had a number of successes in their frequent clashes with the ALN. While these actions sometimes resulted in only a few Muslim casualties, others hit the ALN fairly hard. For example, on 27th September, 105 insurgents were killed in a fight with French troops near Fort MacMahon, another 50 were killed on 18th November near Bou Saada, another 23 were killed on 27th November near Tebessa, 70 were killed and 56 taken prisoner on 9th December on the edge of the Sahara, and on the 22nd of that month, 47 more were killed near Tebessa. French casualties were comparatively light in these and other actions.

These interceptive tactics were very disruptive to the ALN especially in central Algeria, and caused morale to sink. This was demonstrated when a zone commander in the Aures, Adjel Adjoul, with some of his men, surrendered to the French without fighting. This was the first occasion such a thing had happened. While food was no problem for the ALN, as such small numbers could live off the land, it was still short of modern arms and trained men. Such weapons as the insurgents possessed were of many different types, causing both an ammunition and a spare parts replacement problem. The ALN was also in the throes of its reorganization according to the Soummam Conference directive which, together with lack of ammunition, restricted insurgent activity.

As a matter of interest, the often talked about ratio of 'ten to one' being required to defeat insurgents was illustrated in one part of Algeria, when in December (1956) the French had about 23,000 troops in the Greater Kabylie area, opposing about 2,300 insurgent fighters, who were in small groups of between 15 and 30. The insurgents were very much on the defensive, and this was some of the most difficult and rugged terrain in Algeria.

Although the French seemed to be slightly more than holding their own in the shooting battles in the countryside, they had other problems, the main one of which was low morale amongst the Harkis, the Muslim levies and volunteers, and in the Algerian Muslim units, resulting in many desertions, often with arms. Occasionally, their French officers were murdered. There was also trouble in the Algerian Muslim units that had been sent to France and Germany.

Civilian authority had been gradually losing control over Algiers for some time. The city became the scene of daily acts of terrorism and death, and in December 1956 there were some

120 terrorist incidents in the city. The underground ALN, master-minded by Ramdane Abbane, had got a firm grip on the Casbah, a rabbit warren of a Muslim slum, made up of about 20 miles of alleyways and packed with over-crowded houses, in which about 80,000 Muslims lived, of whom French intelligence sources estimated that at least 4,000 were engaged in, or connected with, terrorism in some way. Connecting roofs and secret passages facilitated the escape of terrorists when hard pressed. Encouraged by Ben Khedda, who had been nominated commander of the Algiers Autonomous Zone, and organized by the shrewd Ramdane Abbane, who was in favour of indiscriminate terrorism, the situation got so out of hand that the Prefect of Algiers became completely helpless, and, with the approval of Lacoste, the Resident Minister, called in the army to take action.

In February (1957), the 10th Paratroop Division commanded by General Massu, having a strength of about 10,000, descended suddenly upon the Casbah, and began to root out the ALN underground with ruthless energy. General Massu used informers, their identity hidden by a covering blanket, to pick out terrorists, and then formed small commando units of the turncoats to hunt down their former comrades, allowing them to terrorize Muslims in a similar manner. The paratroops started the 'ilot' system of surveillance and checking personnel, by making one man responsible for a family, and another responsible for a building or house in which there were invariably many families, another for a whole alleyway or street, and so on. In this way they were able to lay their hands on any wanted Muslim in the Casbah within hours. Soon General Massu had a network of informers that eventually rose to about 1,500 in number.

By the end of February, the pressure on the underground ALN in the Casbah was so great that all the members of the CCE and other prominent insurgents, including Ben Khedda and Ramdane Abbane, had fled to the safety of Tunisia. The command of Algiers was handed over to Yecef Saadi.

General Massu's progress continued throughout the year to

such an extent that he completely smashed the ALN fund-raising organization, which obtained money by extortion, and also put out of action the ALN political and military cells in the city. The supporting OPA was badly knocked about. His counter-terrorist commandos, formed of turncoats, eroded into the very framework of the underground movement. Terrorist incidents, such as bomb-throwing, became less frequent, as the entire Muslim population became cowed and chastened.

On 24th September, Yacef Saadi surrendered, and his successor, together with 23 other insurgent terrorists, was killed on 8th October, which more or less ended the ALN underground organization in the city. Although curfews remained and fortified emplacements were still in evidence, in November the ALN was openly admitting failure in the cities, while the French were saying optimistically that the end of the military battle was in sight. General Massu became the hero of the Europeans for his achievement, and his paratroops stayed on in Algiers in a police role, but in decreasing numbers.

The loss of the Battle of Algiers was a severe blow to the FLN and the ALN, and set them back quite a way. Not only in Algiers had things gone badly for them, but in other cities and towns they had suffered reverses, although not always to the same degree, as the 'Direction de la Surveillance du Territoire', the DST, the French security police, became more practised and efficient.

A scapegoat had to be found, and this was Ramdane Abbane, the efficient organizer, who had advocated and organized terrorism in Algiers. He was blamed for the ALN failure, and his star began to wane. But there was more to it than this. Ramdane Abbane had been the organizer of the Soummam Conference and had been prominent in pushing forward the collective leadership principle, which Ben Bella was not too keen on. In fact, if Ben Bella had not been kidnapped when he was, there might have been a split in the FLN on this issue when factions might have formed. As it was, from his place of internment. Ben Bella upbraided Ramdane Abbane for this decision, while in riposte Ramdane Abbane openly accused

F   81

Ben Bella of wanting to assume dictatorial powers, and of failing to honour the agreement made by the 'Club des Neuf' not to take any decision that was not approved by all of them. The principle of collective leadership became established and this issue faded in time, but Belkacem Krim and older insurgent leaders disliked the thrusting, ambitious Ramdane Abbane, and they turned against him. Ramdane Abbane had always been deeply suspicious of the 'Club des Neuf' and in turn was actively disliked by them.

After the failure of the Battle for Algiers, Ramdane Abbane was given a job in connection with procuring arms for the insurgents and getting them into Algeria. He made a favourable arms agreement with Bourguiba, of Tunisia, but after that he quickly faded from prominence, less and less being heard of him until one day in June 1958, an issue of *El Mouadjahed*, the FLN newspaper, noted briefly that he had 'died of wounds the previous month whilst inspecting troops on Algerian territory'. Hardly anything is reliably known about how he received his fatal wounds, which led to speculation as to whether he had been deliberately eliminated by the FLN leadership.

Although he died, or was eliminated, in disgrace and disfavour, Ramdane Abbane had made one vital contribution to the FLN: that of ensuring the principle of collective leadership, which was done at a time when many personalities were striving for individual power, a situation which could only have led to splintering a movement already beset by a powerful rival faction, the MNA, in the uncertain, early days of its struggle.

The French Government of Mollet walked an unsteady tightrope, having to weather the controversial Suez Campaign of November 1956 as well as coming into international friction with countries such as Czechoslovakia, Yugoslavia and Poland over seizures of arms from ships of those countries intended for the ALN in Algeria. In Algeria, it was unpopular with the Europeans who disliked the Government's intention to give the country a new constitution in which they might have only a minority voice. The vacillating and contradictory policy of half-hearted pacification on the one hand and of social, rural, agricultural and economic reform and improvement on the other, satisfied neither side. The French Government was continually embarrassed by the Communist Deputies, although their power and influence declined after the Hungarian Rising of 1956.

The official government policy was to insist that Algeria, being part of France, was a domestic matter, while the efforts of the External Delegation of the FLN were concentrated upon internationalizing the problem. The FLN managed to force a debate on Algeria in January (1957). Immediately prior to this, on 9th January, Mollet issued a 'declaration of intention' on Algeria, which contained a few new proposals, including one that free elections could take place under foreign supervision and that the administration should be largely decentralized. This was coldly received by both Europeans and Muslims in Algeria, and was publicly rejected by the FLN. During the period of the Mollet Government the Europeans increased their political strength.

Early in January (1957), the Faure Conspiracy was brought to light when General Faure, second-in-command of the Algiers Region, was awarded 30 days' confinement[1] for being in contact with extremist European elements, who began to be known as 'Ultras'. It is believed that he was involved in a plot to kidnap Lacoste, the Resident Minister, and place a military government in power in Algeria. This attempted coup was nipped in the bud.

On the 16th of the same month there was an attempt on the life of General Salan, the supreme military commander in Algeria, who had been appointed the previous November, and who was considered by the Ultras to be too soft. Two bazooka shots were fired by Ultras into his office at Army headquarters

---

[1] After spending two weeks in confinement, General Faure was given a command in Germany. In July 1958, he returned to Algeria, being appointed to command the Kabylie Region. It is a peculiarity of the French military system that a senior officer can be arrested and confined, or perhaps suspended from duty for an offence, and then continue with his military career afterwards.

in Algiers from a neighbouring rooftop. General Salan was out of the room at the time, but one of his staff was killed. Nine people were eventually arrested for this incident, but there was considerable delay in bringing them to trial. This murder attempt was thought to be part of a much larger plot, directed by a mysterious 'Staff of Six', which was alleged by some of the arrested persons to include General Cogny and Soustelle. General Cogny denied this, but Soustelle's explanation was evasive. General Salan was unpopular with the Europeans and distrusted by them, and they hoped that General Cogny would become the supreme military commander in his place. One suggestion was that the bazooka attempt was the result of impatience, which may have been true.

These two incidents illustrated the depth of feeling amongst the Europeans, who were alarmed as to what their future might be, and showed to what lengths the Ultras were prepared to go. The Ultras gathered strength and sought to win the army to their cause, bitterly criticizing French Government measures and policy. On 9th June, an explosion in a European dance hall killed 10 and injured 80 Europeans. This set off a wave of anti-Muslim terrorism, and two days later, at the funeral of the victims, European mobs shouted 'Massu to Power'.

Both France and the FLN tried to gain full American support, but both failed, though not altogether. American aid and loans to France continued, to the anxiety, not only of the FLN, but also of Tunisia and Morocco; nevertheless America, while not liking the way France was handling her Algerian problem, was concerned lest the Europeans seize power from a weak French Government and establish in Algeria a minority white rule similar to that in South Africa. In March 1957, Vice-President Nixon visited both Morocco and Tunisia, when both the Sultan and Bourguiba tried to win him over, pressing the idea of forcing France, through threat of economic penalties, to give Algeria gradual independence, with a view to that country becoming part of a federated Magreb. This move was not successful.

The FLN held a press conference in Tunis in the same month

(March) when several appointments were announced. Mohammed Lamine-Debaghine was named head of the External Delegation. A doctor, formerly of the PPA in 1943 when a medical
student, he was an early prominent member of CRUA, joining
the FLN in 1955. Arrested in June 1955, and later released to
house arrest, he escaped to Paris and then to Cairo.

The following month, April, the External Delegation moved
from Cairo to Tunis. This was considered to be a diplomatic
triumph for Bourguiba, President of Tunisia, and was seen partly
as a means of reducing Egyptian influence on FLN affairs, and
partly to give support to Bourguiba in his scheme for a Greater
Magreb — which, of course, he would dominate. Belkacem Krim
handed over his Wilaya (Kabylie), to which he returned briefly
when the Battle of Algiers began, to Said Mohammed, and went
to Tunis as the liaison officer between the External Delegation
and the ALN inside Algeria. Amar Ouamrane, of Wilaya IV,
who had just been on an unsuccessful mission to the still unsettled Wilaya I, where Omar Ben Boulaid held uneasy sway,
was put in charge of obtaining arms and supplies, a job formerly
held by Ramdane Abbane.

The move of the External Delegation to Tunisia caused that
country, secure from French military intervention in its internal
affairs, to become a refuge, base and training centre for the
ALN. Tunisian army barracks and camps, together with some
transport, were handed over to the ALN. A plan was worked
out that preserved Tunisian dignity, while at the same time
giving maximum help to the ALN. The Tunisian National
Guard, the tiny regular army, carried arms and supplies to the
western part of the country where they were handed over to the
ALN. Certain villages became exchange centres. Europeans
were gradually ordered to move from certain sections of western
Tunisia. Generally, ALN soldiers in uniform were kept away
from towns and large villages.

Tunisia became known as the Eastern Base, and by the end of
the year there were over 30,000 ALN troops in the country,
being mainly raw recruits in training, together with wounded.
All ALN wounded were openly treated in Tunisian hospitals,

the excuse being that this was merely a humanitarian act that had nothing to do with the war. It has been said that the Tunisian authorities were helpless, being too weak to prevent what was happening, and merely floated with the tide. This was largely true, but relations with the FLN remained good, and the Tunisians did more than they need have done. The FLN was given Tunisian diplomatic sponsorship, but perhaps this good deed was tinged with the desire to out-smart Egypt. Also, the tiny Tunisian National Guard put to an end the activities of Larbi Taleb, a free-lance smuggler and bandit who was giving the ALN considerable trouble in Tunisia and seizing its supplies *en route*. In addition, Tunisia became flooded with Muslim refugees from Algeria, who were destitute and had to be fed and looked after.[1]

FLN relations with Morocco were not quite so easy or good, and although ALN camps and bases had been set up near the Algerian border inside Morocco, there were restrictions and difficulties. Unlike Bourguiba, who was physically unable to prevent what was happening in his country, the Sultan of Morocco, having a larger army, had the means to take drastic action against the ALN should he choose to use it. Eventually a conference was held in Tangiers, attended by representatives of the FLN, Morocco and Tunisia, to define common interests of the three, after which relations between the FLN and the Sultan improved. The ALN bases in eastern Morocco became known as the Western Base.[2]

Both Morocco and Tunisia had obtained independence from France on favourable terms, and both wished to keep French contacts and to continue to receive French aid. But their assistance to the FLN caused France to restrict financial help, and there was an exodus of French citizens, who had much needed money and skills. These two countries had another worry. The temptation to the French Army to cross the border and smash

---

[1] By the end of 1957, Muslim Algerian refugees in Tunisia numbered more than 60,000.

[2] By the end of 1957 there were about 40,000 Muslim Algerian refugees in Morocco.

the ALN bases must have been very great, especially as the French Army had the ability to do this. Should this have happened to Tunisia, for example, her achievement in gaining independence would have been nullified and the country would have had to start fighting for this objective all over again. The same would be the case for Morocco. The worrying question was whether the French Army would remain on the Algerian side of the borders in the face of provocation of insurgent attacks from the Eastern and Western Bases. The French Army at times mildly exercised the 'right of hot pursuit'. In April 1957, about 80,000 French troops still remained in Tunisia.

Both the Sultan of Morocco and President Bourguiba of Tunisia were disappointed when Lamine-Debaghine was appointed head of the FLN External Delegation, as they favoured Ferhat Abbas, whom they considered a moderate. In September, Bourguiba declared a State of Emergency in his country because of the number of frontier incidents.

The Tunisian National Guard had expanded from about 3,000 to 6,200 on achieving independence, but half were without arms. It was completely unable to stem any invasion from Algeria, as indeed was the ALN in Tunisia, which was neither well enough trained or armed. France was asked by Tunisia to supply certain arms for the National Guard, but refused, fearing they might fall into insurgent hands. President Bourguiba then asked America and Britain, threatening to seek Soviet assistance if he did not obtain enough infantry weapons for his small army. Eventually, in November, both America and Britain sent small, token quantities of arms[1] to Tunisia, but this caused friction between those two countries and France. As a counter, and anxious about the way the insurrection was going for the ALN, which on the whole had had a bad year, President Bourguiba hopefully offered his 'good offices' to try and bring about a cease-fire in Algeria. He tried always to walk the diplomatic tight-rope, and to be friends with France, Egypt, the FLN, America and Britain.

[1] America provided about 500 rifles and some ammunition, and Britain 70 Bren guns, 350 Sterling sub-machine-guns and some ammunition.

87

A number of incidents had occurred on the Algerian border with Libya, where arms were smuggled through from Egypt by camel caravans. But in October 1957 the French accepted a Libyan proposal to investigate and de-limit certain sections of this frontier. Incidents continued, but in less number as the weight and focus of arms supply were directed on to Tunisia.

During 1957, the total strength of the ALN rose to probably just over 40,000 uniformed fighters, of whom some 25,000 were outside Algeria. Many of the latter were recruits, who were now coming forward more willingly, and who were at once packed off on a stiff two-month basic training course at the Eastern Base. This meant that gradually more trained, or semi-trained, soldiers became available. Up until this point no Algerian Muslim recruits had been refused. The uniformed part of the ALN rose in strength only slowly owing to shortage of arms, but all volunteers were taken, and if there were no vacancies in the regular element, the Moujahidines, they were put into either the Moussebilines (the regional element) or the Fidayines (the village militia) until they were required, which in practice meant when arms became available. Together the Moussebilines and the Fidayines probably totalled about 90,000, making an overall ALN strength, of all elements, of about 130,000 of whom only a tiny percentage were women. This was the maximum strength, which the ALN succeeded in holding for only a few months.

This strength fitted in with the view of the Committee of Co-ordination and Execution that the time was rapidly approaching for a change in the pattern of the war, and that as soon as possible the ALN should move on a stage in the progression, and practise mobile warfare against the French Army. The CCE considered that the ALN was deep in the throes of the protracted stage of insurgent warfare. More men and more arms, and too much emphasis on the French political weaknesses and French comparative military inactivity, most probably prompted this decision. Certainly it was a misguided and unsound one that resulted in heavy ALN casualties. Another cause prompting the ALN to change to larger formations was the

need—caused by the internationalization of the FLN struggle—
to demonstrate its power and ability to operate inside Algeria.
By autumn 1957, the ALN had planned to enlarge its battalions to 600 men, (There were hardly any women in the
combatant units.) The ALN battalions began to receive more
modern arms, such as Brownings, automatic weapons, 81 mm.
mortars, and both 30 mm. and 50 mm. machine-guns. They
also became reasonably efficient, but the CCE overlooked the
fact that the French Army opposing them had armour, artillery
and mobility in the form of vehicles and aircraft. For example,
the French had over 200 helicopters. Also, larger ALN units
were less mobile and flexible. This scheme to increase the size of
ALN field units had to be modified mainly owing to shortage of
competent officers, and beginning in the winter, battalions were
made up to a strength of about 380 officers and men, modelled
on those of the French Army in which so many of the ALN
officers had served in Indo-China. This reorganization was in
preparation for an offensive against the French Army in the
spring (1958).

In June 1957, Mahmoud Cherif, a former officer in the
Spahis, who had fought for the French in Indo-China, became
the commander of Wilaya V. Mahmoud Cherif was efficient
and capable, and soon developed into the strong man of
Western Algeria. In Wilaya II, Abdellah Ben Tobbal had replaced Youssef Zighout, who had been killed shortly after the
Soummam Conference.

Although there were many clashes with French troops, the
ALN was fully engaged in combating the armed bands of
the MNA, which were springing into action in certain parts of
the country under the name of the 'National Army of the Algerian People'. The ALN suffered many casualties in this bitter,
fratricidal fighting. There were many reprisals, and a notorious
one occurred on 28th May (1957), when the ALN killed the male
inhabitants, about 300 in all, of a village in Kabylie, because
they had accepted MNA protection. The ALN had threatened
reprisals to any Muslim asking for or accepting MNA protection, and the MNA had issued similar counter threats to anyone

supporting the ALN. This was but one incident; there were others, and in fact, it may be true to say that for several months the MNA caused more casualties to the ALN than did the French Army, but this situation was reversed as the ALN obtained more and better arms.

During 1957, there were many clashes between French and ALN troops, and generally the ALN got the worst of the encounters, suffering heavy casualties. June was a bad month for the ALN, and on the 4th and 5th, 125 insurgents were killed in a fight near Fort MacMahon, and another 48 near Tlemcen on the 14th. On the 15th, an ALN battalion was caught trying to cross into Algeria from Tunisia, losing over 205 men killed. A few days later, in a combined French air and ground sweep in the Collo Peninsula, which despite French efforts remained a strong insurgent centre, 100 ALN soldiers were killed near Djidjelli.

July was a quiet month as the ALN soldiers avoided fighting if possible, except on the edge of the Sahara Desert, to prevent unnecessary damage to growing crops. In August there were more fighting and heavy ALN casualties, the French claiming to have killed, captured or wounded 800 insurgents in 200 minor engagements in the first ten days of the month. On the 13th, 98 ALN soldiers were killed near Tebessa, and on the 31st another 107 in the Aures Mountains. French forces were sometimes caught in unfavourable circumstances with disastrous results, but not nearly so often.

As ALN units became larger and better armed they became bolder and major engagements were fought in the Collo Peninsula, Kabylie, the Ouarsenis and Oran Province. There was fighting at times in the Nementcha Mountains and along the Tunisian frontier area.

The quadrillage strategy lay heavily on the ALN network, restricting activity. It was curbing, but not crushing, the insurrection. The main drawback was that it required so many troops in static roles. There were never more than about 20,000 French troops available for mobile operations to hunt out the ALN fighters at large in Algeria, which may have amounted to about 15,000 or so. Made up of French paratroops, French volunteer regiments and Foreign Legion units, the interception measures of this mobile force had a dismaying effect on the ALN, especially in the central parts of the country. The French had the advantage of good mobility, both on land and in the air, while the ALN did not even have vehicles and had to rely upon their feet.

Like the ALN, the French also suffered casualties, and in the early days of August, 76 French soldiers were killed in four days' fighting, 10 were killed in ambush near Orléansville, and on the 13th another seven were killed near Laghouat. This was the deadly pattern, as month followed month. Estimates of French military casualties from the outbreak of the insurrection until 31st October (1957)—that is, for the first three years of the war—were 3,700 killed, 6,000 wounded and 650 missing, but these figures included French-Muslim troops and auxiliaries. (The desertion rate of Algerian Muslims serving with the French Army was then approximately 200 a month.) These figures do not include Muslim civilians, of whom probably 6,200 were killed, 4,100 injured and 2,100 missing in the same period.

September saw the first ALN surrenders, without fighting, of the war so far, when on the 7th, a platoon of 21 men gave themselves up. Others, in smaller batches and ones and twos, did the same when faced with heavy odds, a thing that had not happened before, as the insurgents, when cornered, had hitherto invariably fought to the death. Between 9th October and the 12th, 108 insurgents in various parts of the country surrendered, with their arms, to the French forces. This new trend was perhaps partly due to lower morale and partly due to weaker material.

However, this was by no means one-sided, and Muslims serving in French units, or in the French service, continued to desert, many with arms, sometimes after killing their officers who had mistakenly trusted and believed in them to the fatal end. For example, on 17th October, 60 Muslims of the Camel Corps near Timimoun mutinied, murdered their eight French officers and joined the ALN with their arms, camels and equipment. There were other similar incidents.

In September, the French completed the Morice Barrage,[1] a 200-mile mined and electrified barrier along the Tunisian frontier, from Bône to El-Ma-El-Aboid, south of Tebessa. The zone between this point and Negrine, on the edge of the Sahara, was controlled by radar, which gave warning of the approach of ALN troops. This blockade was very effective and restricted ALN movement across the border, driving it to desperation tactics and to recklessly risking men's lives to get them into Algeria and out again. On 4th November an insurgent convoy was intercepted attempting to get through the Morice Barrage near Tebessa, losing 45 men killed, while another 48 were killed on 1st December in similar circumstances near Souk-Ahras. This caused the ALN units to make detours farther south, and on 7th December 121 were killed near El-Ma-El-Aboid, 75 insurgents were killed in battle near Guelma on the 10th, and 70 more near Tebessa on the 19th—and so on.

Other engagements occurring towards the end of 1957 that can be quoted include an ALN ambush in Ouarsenis (between Relizane and Tiaret), a growing centre of ALN activity, in which nine French soldiers were killed, but in ensuing operations, over 40 insurgent dead were counted. Forty-one insurgents were killed about 20 miles south of Algiers on 29th/30th November in the Collo Peninsula, and over 160 men in the Kabylie and Constantine areas during the first two weeks of December. These typical examples indicate that the war was being hard fought in most parts of Algeria, and that contrary to popular belief in an unfavourable section of the European Press and the blatant and often inaccurate FLN propaganda, the ALN was having a rough time and suffering a heavy and serious drain on manpower that was not readily appreciated.

For the first three years of the war, until 31st October, unofficial estimates indicated that the ALN had lost over 30,000 killed and 13,000 captured. This meant, as these figures are largely correct, that the ALN had been almost wiped out once.

[1] Named after the then Minister of Defence, André Morice.

It is not how low ALN morale was that is amazing, but how in the face of such casualties recruits could still be produced and encouraged to fight.

In general from the French point of view the situation greatly improved during 1957, and in August the Defence Minister decided to reduce the number of French troops in Algeria by 70,000 by the end of the following year, and he reduced the (then) term of military service from 27 months to two years. This was despite the fact that the quadrillage system caused the mobile reserve to be so small.

In Algeria the ALN was winning its battle against the MNA, although it could not completely defeat and eliminate its rival, but in France the FLN had less success. The underground struggle between the two continued, especially in Paris. From October 1956 until October 1957, it was estimated that over 550 Algerian Muslims were killed and over 2,200 wounded in France by rival terrorist organizations. Many were tortured. This pattern continued, and, for example, on an average about two Algerians a day were killed in Paris alone. Not only were the FLN and the MNA fighting each other, but also Muslim racketeers and gangsters stepped into the conflict practising extortion under the guise of nationalism, and gangs of thugs and nationalist groups desperately fought each other.

The External Delegation continued to do well in the diplomatic and political fields, but was forced to take a realistic look at how events were shaping in Algeria. In August 1957, the second FLN Congress was held in Cairo, which caused President Bourguiba to become a little apprehensive that President Nasser might regain all influence over the FLN. But he need not have worried as the FLN was merely being diplomatic. At this Congress Lamine-Debaghine was confirmed as head of the External Delegation. The CNRA, virtually the governing committee, was expanded from 34 to 54 members, but this time their names were not made public. The CCE also expanded to become a 14-man executive committee.

The Congress was deeply disturbed by the failure of the ALN in the Battle of Algiers. A few months earlier the leaders of the

FLN had optimistically thought that the victorious end of the struggle was in sight. Now they realized they had been wrong, and that a long arduous campaign lay ahead, calling for hard work and careful planning. Increased aid was requested from Middle East countries, and even Saudi Arabia, a country disliked by the FLN because of its régime, was approached for this purpose.

In December, FLN representatives attended the Afro-Asian Conference held in Cairo, when they put their case forward. Also, at the United Nations, Mohammed Yazid kept the FLN cause continually to the forefront.

Another factor now began to protrude into the Algerian struggle: oil, which brought with it dreams of riches and power. The first discovery of oil in Algeria in reasonable commercial quantity was made early in 1956, in the Edjele region near the Libyan border. A second important find was announced in June the same year at Tiguentourine, some 40 miles west of Edjele. But the largest find of all was discovered in the December, at Hassi Massaoud, with a (then) estimated minimum reserve of 100 million metric tons. Further oil deposits were found in May and June 1957. Also discovered were large deposits of natural gas, iron ore and other minerals, such as manganese.

Oil installations were set up, pipe and railway lines constructed, and preparations made to ship oil to France. The first cargo of Algerian oil left Philippeville for that country on 4th March 1958. The vulnerability of the oil pipelines and installations was realized by the insurgents, and minor attacks and sabotage had begun in October (1957). The ALN announced the formation of a 'Saharan Front', obviously designed to hamper the flow of oil. On 6th November 1957 a party of oil prospectors and their military escort were ambushed and 16 of them killed near Timimoun. Paratroops were flown to the area, and sought out and killed over 40 insurgents during the ensuing days. On 10th December the French stated that although there still remained about 60 ALN fighters in the district, the so-called Saharan Front had been eliminated. Even so, rail communication between the oil fields and the coast was cut on several occasions.

The French Army, having embarked upon psychological warfare, mildly and almost timidly, began to develop and expand this medium. With Lacoste's approval, in November 1957 the 5th Bureau (the name for the Psychological Warfare Section of the French Army) was established and encouraged to function. Senior and older officers, being more conservative and perhaps concerned with prospects of promotion and stability, viewed this type of warfare with distaste and had as little to do with it as possible, but younger officers, especially many in the middle grade bracket, saw the potentialities and appreciated its importance. A psychological warfare centre was created through which all new officer arrivals from France to Algeria had to pass. At this centre they were familiarized with subversive warfare methods and ways to combat it.

The officers of both the SAS (Sections Administratives Specialisées) and the SAU (Sections Administratives Urbaines) became political propagandists, acutely aware of the importance of winning a person's mind and allegiance. The SAS and the SAU had been formed from the old Arab Bureau in 1955 and only specially selected officers were recruited and trained to work with Muslim auxiliaries. The SAU was an organization that worked in towns. At first the SAS and the SAU were under civil control, but as they expanded and contained more and more army officers, the military authorities took over complete direction. There was some friction between the SAS and the Army, as the SAS insisted that it built up good will, while the Army simply destroyed it.

The Army also formed small special psychological detachments, the 'Détachements Opérationnels de Protection', the DOP, for particular tasks. A stratum within the French Army became very psychologically-minded, justifying its actions by the conviction that the Army was the only unifying factor between a rebellious Algeria and a leaderless France, which filled a sort of power vacuum.

Psychological warfare methods, now commonly thought of as 'brain-washing', made notorious by the Communists of Asia, were applied to Algerian Muslims in internment camps and amongst groups of displaced persons. The system was first of all to break down their existing beliefs and cause the subjects to lose faith in the FLN ideals, aims and leaders. Then they were given a new belief to replace them, the belief in a French-Muslim Algeria. The third stage was to fit the newly orientated Algerian-Muslim into the country socially and economically. Many leaves were taken from Communist handbooks on the subject, and the processes were applied with plenty of hard work and barrages of indoctrination. All day long loud-speakers bombarded the victims with slogans, and they had to read, or be read, pamphlets, which were discussed under controlled chairmanship. There were rewards for improvement and 'correct thinking', and the more responsive were elected 'prefects'. These processes had surprising, and frightening, success. A howl of protest was raised by the French Communists, all Arab states and some Communist countries.

Another feature that raised criticism was that Lacoste, the Resident Minister, directed French troops, in their letters home, to correct misconceptions about Algeria. This led to pressures and 'guidance' on what the men wrote from their Commanding Officers.

Subverting the ALN and other insurgent and bandit groups and persuading them to fight with the French against the ALN was another psychological method that was tried with some success in the second half of 1957, causing for a time anxiety and embarrassment to the insurgent army. Some of the groups that were persuaded to turn their coats were permitted to remain under their own leaders in a semi-autonomous role to co-operate with French troops against the insurgents. In return, the French provided arms, ammunition and money.

Si Cherif, a former ALN battalion commander, went over to the French side with 500 men in July 1957, and fought well for them in the Medea region. Another turn-coat, who gave good service to the French, was Belhadj Djilal, also a former ALN battalion commander. He fought the ALN in the Orléansville sector.

The best psychological success in this sphere was obtaining

the services of Mohammed Bellounis, the virtual commander of the National Army of the Algerian People, the military arm of the MNA. Mohammed Bellounis had fought both the French and the ALN in the areas of the Grand Kabylie and the Djurdjura Mountains since 1955, and had built up a small army of about 4,500 armed fighters, the bulk of the field force of the MNA. By an agreement with the French, Mohammed Bellounis in November 1957 was given arms and money and entrusted with the responsibility for operating against the ALN in the region of Aumale, Bou Saada and Aflou. With vicious energy he fought the ALN, and also practised torture and extortion in a big way, terrorizing the inhabitants in the region. This was a sharp setback for the ALN in that part of central Algeria.

By this time a darker aspect of the war, torture, was emerging. There was also deliberate brutality to intimidate prisoners. There had been rumours and allegations for some time that the French Army had been indulging in torture and eventually a commission was appointed to report on the matter, known as the 'Commission de Sauvegarde des droits et des libertés individuels', the 'Safeguard Commission'. Its formation was announced on 5th April 1957, and it submitted a report in the September of that year.

The findings of the Safeguard Commission were 'leaked' by *L'Express* in the December. The report had said that there was no general system or approval of torture of prisoners in the French Army in Algeria, but there had been many isolated incidents, all of which had been inquired into, when officers or soldiers were punished if found guilty. In the (then) eight large internment camps, housing some 6,000 Muslims[1] the Safeguard Commission found matters satisfactory. The provocation on the French side was great, especially when dealing with terrorists, as if a captured terrorist could be persuaded to talk, other terrorists could be arrested, and so prevented from killing many people. If the arrested terrorist did not talk, then a number of people were inevitably bound to die at the hands of his colleagues still at large. The French Army faced a terrible choice.

[1] There were also over 5,000 Algerian Muslims under 'house arrest'.

On the ALN side of the fence there was no doubt—and frequent material evidence was available—that fiendishly cruel torture was practised, when lips, noses and other parts of the body were cut off or mutilated, before death. Captured French soldiers were not excluded from this inhuman treatment, and so again there was great provocation.

The French Navy maintained a watch off Algerian shores for ships carrying contraband arms for the insurgents. On 18th January 1958, for example, a Yugoslav ship *en route* to Casablanca was stopped and found to be carrying enough arms[1] to equip about half a dozen ALN battalions. These arms, which were seized by the French, included 350 bangalore torpedoes, presumably for use to blow gaps in the electrified barriers erected along parts of the Moroccan and Tunisian frontiers. The arms were intended for the Western Base to equip newly-forming ALN units. Yugoslavia lodged a protest, but the French stood firm, and this attitude probably made the Iron Curtain countries supplying arms to the FLN more cautious in their methods of delivery.

If there was an international outcry when a Yugoslav ship was stopped on the high seas, there was a far bigger one on 8th February 1958 when French aircraft bombed and machine-gunned the Tunisian border village of Sakiet[2] on a market day, killing 79 people and wounding another 130. Women and children were amongst the dead and wounded. The Tunisians made propaganda capital of this incident, rushing Red Cross representatives to Sakiet immediately after the air raid to see the damage, dead and wounded. Journalists were brought there the next day, and diplomatic representatives of several countries were taken sightseeing to Sakiet on the 10th. The 15,000 French troops still in Tunisia were confined to barracks and attempts were made to cut off their supplies, water and electricity by individual Tunisians. Over 600 French settlers in Tunisia were moved away from the border zone.

---

[1] The ship carried about 55 tons of arms and 95 tons of ammunition, all destined for the FLN in Morocco.

[2] In full, Sakiet Sidi Youssef.

Tunisia trumpeted loudly, saying that Sakiet was a peaceful village and that the French Air Force had deliberately bombed women and children. The French Government denied authorizing this bombing, but on inquiry supported the action, declaring that Sakiet was an ALN transit and intelligence centre, filled with ALN soldiers. No Minister's approval for this raid had been sought, or given. The French military command had again acted on its own initiative without consulting the political leaders responsible.

The French had violated Tunisian territory on this occasion, but it had serious provocation. The frontier in this area had been a troubled one for some months, the French alleging that there had been 84 violations, of which about 26 were very close to Sakiet, off the Algerian frontier with Tunisia between 1st July 1957 and 7th February 1958, while the Tunisians alleged over 50 French violations of their frontier in the same period. On 11th January, a French patrol was ambushed in Algerian territory, about four miles from Sakiet, which was about 700 metres from the actual border, when 16 soldiers were killed and another four taken prisoner. The French believed that the prisoners had been taken into Tunisia, and an emissary, a serving general, was sent to President Bourguiba to ask him for their release, but Bourguiba would not see him. Later, by arrangement with the FLN, Red Cross representatives visited the four French prisoners on Algerian territory, but it was thought that they had been taken there specially and the visit laid on for propaganda purposes.

In the seven months previous to the Sakiet bombing, French aircraft had been fired upon 30 times from the Tunisian side of the border, mainly near Sakiet, and 11 had been hit and two forced down. French aircraft were fired on by anti-aircraft guns from the village on 30th January, and again from the same place on 7th February. On 7th February, the French warned the Tunisian military authorities that any more attacks of this nature on her aircraft would result in reprisals. On the morning of the 8th, a French aircraft was fired upon from Sakiet and forced to land. This provocation lay behind the much publicized bombing of Sakiet.

The Sakiet Incident released a renewed wave of ALN attacks throughout Algeria, and February was a bad month for the French forces, which lost 297 killed in action (as compared with 207 killed during the previous February). But these attacks cost the insurgents nearly 2,600 dead. There had been, on average, about 2,000 incidents, big and small, a month in Algeria throughout 1957.

Both America and Britain were deeply concerned lest the fighting in Algeria spread to Tunisia, and both offered their 'good offices' to try to bring about negotiations between France and Tunisia. Lack of NATO military strength in Europe was a worry to Western Powers, and the previous month (January) America had just granted France $655 million credits, with the object of helping her economy and encouraging her to allow French troops to remain in Germany.

Despite increasing ALN advantages, added world sympathy for the FLN cause, a weak French Government and an unruly Ultra European influence, the French Army in Algeria had succeeded in holding down the ALN since August 1956, and killing over 2,000 insurgents a month, out of a probable constant armed and uniformed fighting strength within the country of about 15,000. Morale in the ALN could not be said to be high.

CHAPTER 5

General de Gaulle Returns to Power
May 1958

Loss of respect and authority by a series of unsettled, weak Governments, the many stresses they had to face both from within and without and the way in which they dealt with the nation's problems, caused a clamour to arise, first voiced only by a minority, and then by increasing numbers in crescendo, for the return of General de Gaulle to take over the Government of France. Leader of the wartime Free French Movement, and formerly a Prime Minister, de Gaulle had held no public office since January 1946 when, disgusted by the aims and ambitions of some of the politicians, he abruptly resigned. He formed his own party, the Rally of the French People, the RFP, but withdrew from its leadership in 1953, since when he had not been active in French political life. Persistently he rejected hints and offers to re-enter politics, remaining on the sidelines cloaked in immense prestige. Although he had a small number of ardent supporters, there were many in the nation, for one reason or another, who disliked the idea of his returning to power, especially the Communists.

In January 1958, the Government of Gaillard became increasingly unpopular with the Europeans in Algeria when it ratified the 'loi cadre' for Algeria. Previously, this measure had been rejected by the French Assembly in September (1957), but it had been again presented in a slightly different form. Under the 'loi cadre' Algeria was to be an integral part of France, but made up of federated territories, each to administer its own affairs. Moreover, it provided for an electoral assembly that could only lead to eventual Muslim control, a fact that angered the Europeans, who, prompted by Ultra elements, were ripe for mischief and violent change.

The Gaillard Government was plagued throughout February and March by international and internal pressures, approbation and dissent, resulting from the Sakiet Incident. Gaillard had not known in advance of the occurrence, but since had refused to reprimand those responsible. The Communists, as usual, wanted peace, but a strong right-wing element demanded that the war in Algeria be pursued more vigorously and was against restoring the abruptly broken diplomatic relations with Tunisia.

The Anglo-American 'good offices' mission, which worked to persuade France and Tunisia to enter into negotiations over the Sakiet Incident, was extremely unpopular in France, and for some time had little success. In fact, America had to hint of possible negotiations with the FLN if France would not co-operate, before Gaillard reluctantly fell in with that country's wishes. This proved to be his downfall, as the greater part of the political 'centre' in France resented outside interference, and on 15th April he fell from office.

Gaillard was asked by President Coty to carry on as caretaker Prime Minister until a new Government was formed, but this proved a difficulty, and France was literally without effective government for about four weeks, until Pierre Pflimlin agreed to form one, which was due to be approved by the National Assembly on 13th May. Already, on 26th April, there had been demonstrations by the Europeans in Algiers against the possible formation of a government by Pflimlin, as it was suspected that he favoured negotiations with the FLN.

There were several plots afoot in seething Algiers, some of greater and some of lesser importance. The main one perhaps was that instigated and organized by Léon Delbecque,[1] a Gaullist Deputy, who had recently been principal private secretary to a Minister of Defence. He frequently visited Algeria,

[1] Delbecque had been in the army in Algeria between 1956 and 1958, serving for a brief period in the Black Commandos.

during which he had made contacts with both leading Ultras and many army officers of varying rank. Delbecque's object was a 'French national resurrection', and he wished to restore General de Gaulle to power, but he had to scheme and plot hard to this end as there were comparatively few Gaullists in Algeria among either the Europeans, who during World War II had sided with Marshal Pétain, or the army officers, the majority of whom had similar views.

Delbecque, who had been in Algeria since January, was planning to launch an insurrection, with the help of the Ultras and the Army, in Algiers on 14th May. As the Ultras were generally solidly anti-Gaullist, he had difficulty in persuading them to co-operate with him, but despite this barrier, he succeeded, and a secret Committee of Public Safety was formed in readiness. He did not think that Pflimlin would succeed in being voted into office as Prime Minister and that France would still be without a government on that date, and so hoped to be able to take advantage of an impasse.[1] On 9th May, Delbecque and Alain de Serigny,[2] a prominent Ultra and the Editor of *L'Echo D'Alger*, after visiting de Gaulle at his home in France, when it is thought they had obtained his moral support for his return to power 'if the people wanted it', flew to Algiers to see Lacoste, the Resident Minister, who was implicated in the early stages of the plot. Delbecque and de Serigny wanted Lacoste to remain in control in Algeria until the political parties in Paris made a truce. The plot was hurried as it was feared that a new French Government might remove Lacoste. Lacoste at first agreed, but had second thoughts, and the next day flew off to Paris where he stayed. Later, Lacoste admitted knowing about this plot, but denied his part in it.

On the same day, the 9th, it had been announced by the FLN that three French prisoners had been shot in reprisal for Algerian Muslim insurgent fighters executed. (They had actually

---

[1] The Ultra demonstrations in Algiers on 26th April were believed to have been a rehearsal for a coup, organized by Delbecque and his fellow plotters.

[2] Alain de Serigny gives an account of his activities in these events in his book *La Révolution du 13 Mai*, published in July 1958.

been shot on 24th April.) This caused great indignation among the Europeans, especially the Ultras and the ex-servicemen's associations. On the 12th, a 'Comité de Vigilance', a Vigilance Committee, formed of 17 patriotic European associations, called for a general strike the next day to coincide with the debate in the National Assembly on Pflimlin's investiture as Prime Minister, and the population of Algiers was urged to demonstrate. The military arranged a wreath-laying ceremony at the War Memorial on the same morning, in memory of the three French soldiers recently shot by the ALN. The Europeans, in the Territorial Units, were to be also represented at the ceremony.

During the five years of war in Algeria the army had gradually assumed almost unlimited powers. The Europeans, especially the Ultras, tried to identify themselves with it through service in the part-time Territorial Units, when they were called up for about one day's service in ten to relieve the army from guard and other static duties. This was a chore, an unwelcome one in most cases, but it gave prestige.

On the morning of the 13th, the Europeans were out in strength in the streets of Algiers, perhaps largely organized by Delbecque to shock the National Assembly into rejecting the Pflimlin Government, and thousands witnessed the wreath-laying ceremony in the centre of the city by senior officers, who included General Massu. The atmosphere was charged and the crowd was pent up with emotion, dissatisfaction and unrest. Before long it was shouting 'The Army to Power' and 'Massu to Power'. The crowd became a mob, which moved spontaneously towards Government House, and becoming unruly, got out of hand and began to damage government buildings. The police lost control and kept in the background. The Ultras were clearly in a dangerous mood.

Seeing what was happening, General Massu telephoned Gaillard in Paris for instructions as to whether he should open fire on the rioters. Gaillard declined to commit himself, saying that he was no longer the Prime Minister, and advised Massu to contact Pflimlin. In his turn, Pflimlin told General Massu that he had not yet been formally elected Prime Minister, and accordingly also declined to give advice or instructions. Massu went to face the European rioters, who were momentarily quietened by his appearance. To them General Massu was their hero who had eliminated the underground insurgent terrorist organization from the city. There were instant shouts of 'Massu to Power', and this cry was widely taken up. The crowd became more orderly when Massu declared that he would place himself at the head of a Committee of Public Safety. Speeches were made and the Ultras placated. Initially, the Committee of Public Safety consisted of four army officers (General Massu and three colonels), seven European civilians and four Muslims. Massu telephoned Lacoste in Paris, saying that this movement was not a coup, but simply to impress the National Assembly that Algeria wished to remain French.

When news of this reached Paris, Gaillard, who was still technically the acting Prime Minister, despite his non-committal words to Massu, telephoned the secretary of the absent Lacoste, to instruct General Salan to assume immediate responsibility for maintaining the Republic's authority in Algeria. General Salan, who tended to be unpopular with the Europeans, and knew it, had kept very much in the background during these events. Massu acknowledged Salan's authority, and announced to the crowd that Soustelle was on his way to Algeria.

General Massu insisted that he had merely stepped forward at the critical moment, accepting the position as head of the Committee of Public Safety on the spur of the moment, knowing his popularity with the Europeans, to try and control something he could not stop. By doing so he estimated that he would prevent bloodshed, disorder and widespread damage. This was probably correct, as Massu may have been a resourceful and quick-thinking soldier, but he lacked political acumen, and he had been swept by events into appearing to become the leader of the rioting crowds. Like many other senior army officers, General Massu had come to believe that the army was the only cohesive force remaining in Algeria and that it was up to it to take appropriate action in emergencies. By the army he meant, of course, the cadre of regular officers, who were convinced that the future of Algeria depended upon them.

Events in Algiers, where the Ultra-led European mobs, under the slender authority of the Committee of Public Safety, were in control of the city, caused consternation in the National Assembly. In the early hours of the 14th Pflimlin was voted in as Prime Minister by a comfortable majority. One of his first acts was to confirm his predecessor's instructions to General Salan. Treading extremely cautiously, the new Government carefully avoided speaking of an 'insurrection in Algiers', and a period of breathless political suspense followed.

The spontaneous acclamation by the crowds of General Massu and his acceptance of the Presidency of the Committee of Public Safety had taken the scheming Delbecque by surprise, and in fact had forestalled his plans by one day. Delbecque, who had been trying secretly to persuade army officers and Europeans to get together, had by this time an embryo insurgent political organization ready and disciplined. It consisted of both army officers, mainly of medium grade, and Europeans, many of whom were Ultras. However, being an astute, quick-witted politician, he at once worked to turn the present events to his own purpose. Pushing himself forward, he became the Vice-President of the Committee of Public Safety, and his followers began to pump out Gaullist propaganda. He traded successfully on the emotional atmosphere of the moment to persuade both the army and the Europeans that General de Gaulle was the man to lead France in this difficult moment.

There were several plots simmering[1] in Algiers about this time, aimed at either changing the Government, the Resident-Minister or the Algerian policy, some advocating military rule in Algeria, but none had come to fruition before the 13th.

On the 14th, President Coty broadcast a message to the army, urging loyalty. Meanwhile, becoming anxious, Generals Salan and Massu sent a communication to Soustelle asking him

[1] *Les 13 Complots du 13 Mai*, by Merry and Serge Bromberger, reveal many interesting factions, plotters and undercurrents.

to hurry, but Soustelle had been prevented from leaving Paris by the police, being taken into 'protective custody' on the new Prime Minister's instructions. The following day, the 15th, was a public holiday, on which little was done in Paris governmental circles. All shipping and telephone communication between France and Algeria, except for official messages, was cut, and in Algeria airfields and public buildings were guarded. The Committee of Public Safety in Algiers was enlarged to 34 members, Delbecque managing to obtain places on the committee for several of his followers. Oran and Constantine began to form similar Committees of Public Safety, and other cities and towns slowly followed suit. These Committees assumed authority, mainly by agreement, although there were instances of friction and opposition from the civil administrators.

Salan, Massu and Delbecque were uneasy at the continued absence of Soustelle, who was now known to be under police restriction. They had in fact expected the National Assembly to reject Pflimlin as Prime Minister and France again to be without a government, when they had hoped to be able to use the political void to their own purpose. That day, the 15th, General de Gaulle made a declaration saying that 'he was ready to assume the powers of the Republic'. This sign gave impetus to Delbecque's campaign to push de Gaulle to the forefront of everyone's minds. That evening, General Salan made a speech to the Europeans and at the end of it added a weak 'Vive de Gaulle', much as a prompted afterthought. This gave the Europeans the idea that the Army wanted de Gaulle to return to power. From that moment in Algiers, and indeed in Algeria, shouts of 'De Gaulle to Power' became progressively louder and more frequent.

On the 16th, in Algiers there occurred unparalleled scenes of fraternization between Muslims and Europeans. These had been organized by the psychological warfare branch of the Army, the 5th Bureau, which suddenly preached complete integration and equality of Muslim and European, both politically and economically. The Muslims flooded down in their thousands from the squalid Casbah to mingle with the Europeans in the streets and in the squares of the city. Also, the army had sent out trucks into the countryside to collect and bring in more Muslims for the same purpose.

The spirit of the moment was such that this gigantic demonstration of fraternization worked impressively. The organizers, the 5th Bureau, pushed hard the theme that the Army was the Muslim's best friend. Delbecque had supported this move so as to emphasize the complete absence of any racialism in the insubordinate upheaval. About 100,000 people demonstrated in front of Government House in support of the Committee of Public Safety, of whom half were Muslim. That day Salan appointed Colonel Godard, a 5th Bureau officer, Director of Internal Security for Algeria.

In Paris there was anxious foreboding. Pflimlin was granted emergency powers for three months in Metropolitan France, and he dissolved four extreme right-wing organizations in the capital. There were many arrests.

Much to the relief of Generals Salan and Massu, and also of Delbecque, late on the 17th Soustelle, having evaded his police escort, arrived in Algiers, where he was given a tremendous welcome by the people. Refusing the position of President of the Committee of Public Safety, Soustelle contented himself with being the 'political adviser to General Salan'. A Gaullist Deputy and a clever politician, he swung the impetus of the Army and European insurrection into Gaullist channels. Much spade work had been done already by Delbecque, but Soustelle, with his prestige and advocacy, gave momentum to the swing in favour of de Gaulle. Soustelle, who had favoured a strong line against the Muslim insurgents and so had gained popularity with the Europeans, felt that under de Gaulle's leadership it would be possible to give Algeria some form of independence within the French constitutional framework. Soon 'Vive de Gaulle' and 'De Gaulle to Power' were on most people's lips, including many army officers. However, the cautious General Salan said little in this respect and would not openly commit himself.

A future policy of complete integration of Muslims and Europeans, all to be French, with the same rights and duties, was enunciated. This had never been said before in so many words. There were hints that wages might be equal for both too, and when doubts were raised as to where the money was coming from, Soustelle pointed to the recent natural oil, gas and mineral discoveries in the Sahara. Ferhat Abbas promptly denounced this as a move against Algerian nationalism—which it certainly was.

After his dramatic announcement of the 15th, General de Gaulle remained silent, watching the tussle between the European insurgents in Algeria and the Government in Paris. He had taken no part in the events in Algiers. On the 19th, he broke his silence and gave a press conference in Paris, attended by pressmen and Gaullist Deputies, totalling in all over 1,200, making it the largest of its kind for many years. He condemned a régime of political parties, but did not criticize the activities of either Soustelle, Salan or Massu. De Gaulle said he was against the use of force, but hinted that if given adequate powers he would come forward and form a government. After this press conference, the wily General Salan came out openly for the return of de Gaulle, and sent a message to Pflimlin saying that he was losing control over Massu's paratroops and could not continue to be responsible for Algeria if de Gaulle was not soon brought to power. The following day, General Salan openly broke with the Pflimlin Government, a move General Massu had publicly made on the 18th.

De Gaulle's utterances, in which moderation seemed to be the theme, may have given some hope to Pflimlin, who with others daily dreaded de Gaulle leading a *coup d'état*. They indicated that he was in favour of assuming power by constitutional methods if possible. On the other hand, the Communists became alarmed at the thought of de Gaulle returning to head a government, and they threatened large-scale strikes if this should occur. In fact, they had already made demonstrations on the 15th, after de Gaulle's first declaration. The next day, the 20th, mass strikes were called for, but out of the some

600,000 members of the Communist-controlled or influenced trade unions in Paris, only about 35,000 withheld their labour, and the protest fizzled out.

On the 23rd, a single Committee of Public Safety for all Algeria and the Sahara (the latter was a separate department under a separate Minister) was formed, consisting of 72 members, under the joint-Presidency of General Massu and Sid Cara, a Muslim Deputy. Soustelle became its political adviser. Most cities and towns in Algeria had by this time their own Committees of Public Safety, which had assumed authority, and on which sat many serving officers. This whole European insurrectionary movement appeared on the face of things to be supported wholeheartedly by the Army, which now, like the Europeans, was calling for the return of General de Gaulle.

The trial of hidden strength and war of nerves between Paris and Algiers continued. For some days there had been strong rumours that the army in Algeria planned to invade Paris to establish a military government. A number of troop-carrying aircraft had been unofficially flown from France to Algeria, where they stood ready under control of the Algerian military command. Pflimlin was in a state of helpless inactivity. The loyalty of the army in France in such a contingency was doubtful, as the senior officers were not sure their orders would be obeyed should General Massu's paratroops descend on the capital. It was also rumoured that certain generals and other officers in France had pledged their support and had indicated that they would aid General Massu if he attempted an airborne take-over of Paris. Already on the 17th, General Ely, Chief of Staff of the Armed Forces, had resigned rather than have to order French soldiers to fire on other French soldiers. He was replaced by General Lorillot, who was General Salan's predecessor in Algeria, but this appointment did not give any greater confidence.

The only forces the Government could rely upon were the police, who in all numbered about 280,000, most of whom were armed. They were used to guard airfields, on which were laid out coils of barbed wire to obstruct any aircraft trying to land,

and other likely landing places, and were mainly concentrated in and around Paris itself. The police were granted emergency powers of arrest and detention, and censorship was imposed on the Press.

A plan to invade the Capital from Algeria existed, but it was a makeshift and impromptu one. Known as 'Opération Résurrection', it was widely discussed in military circles in Algeria, but it could hardly be said to have been a sound, master plan. Exactly how much of it was bluff and how much was concrete fact is hard to say exactly. Most probably it was a mixture of both, with which the Algerian generals and the All Algerian Committee of Public Safety hoped to stampede Pflimlin's Government into giving in to their demands, which were now unitedly that General de Gaulle must return to power.

At first French officers had not been involved with political affairs, nor were the majority of them really interested. They were all acutely disappointed by the loss of Indo-China, which they put down to the ineptitude, blundering and lack of support from the politicians, and when they saw similar mismanagement in Algeria discontent within the officer cadre grew, becoming apparent the previous year (1957). By allowing, and even encouraging, the Army to indulge in psychological warfare, Mollet had introduced officers to politics, and a large number of them found it to be a fascinating game indeed. In Algeria they had not originally particularly liked the Europeans, their attitudes or views, but events had increasingly thrown the Army into sympathy with them. Moreover, senior army officers had been occasionally asked their political opinions on certain events, and then after a while they came to proffer them unasked. The driving political influence in the army consisted of a number of medium grade and junior officers, especially a group of colonels, who had tasted politics and found it to their liking. Overnight, under the urging of Soustelle, they had become Gaullists.

General Salan, the most senior serving officer in Algeria, was distrusted by most army officers, as he had a reputation as an intriguer, and was suspected of being in league, or at least in secret contact, with several Paris politicians of different persuasions. He was therefore to some extent isolated and left out of their plans by the scheming colonels. There was also a limit as to how far the army plotters trusted and confided in General Massu. In fact both Salan and Massu were to a large degree figureheads, simply going along with the tide, riding the crest of the wave precariously, and having little real control over events. They had committed themselves openly, and now could do no other.

On 24th May, French paratroops in transport aircraft flew from Algeria to Corsica, where, together with local leaders and politicians, they took over Ajaccio, the capital of the island. A Committee of Public Safety was formed, which called for General de Gaulle to take over the French Government. This coup had been planned in Algeria, and Delbecque, who flew over to Corsica with the paratroops, had been one of its instigators. More alarming still, 160 policemen from France who had been specially sent over to Corsica to restore order, joined the rebels. France was clearly desperately close to anarchy and civil war. All forms of communication between France and Algeria were cut completely, the Government optimistically estimating that the army in Algeria could not carry on for more than a fortnight without further supplies from France. On the 25th, all broadcasts from Algeria were jammed in France.

Suspense reached a high nerve-racking pitch. In Algeria everyone shouted loudly for General de Gaulle. In Paris, where daily the citizens expected an airborne invasion of French paratroops from Algeria, the politicians haggled over terms, being reluctant to allow de Gaulle any extra powers should they not be able to prevent him becoming leader of the Government. On the other hand, de Gaulle consistently refused to step forward, except on his own terms.

On the 24th, a message reached General de Gaulle that the generals in Algeria could not delay their projected invasion of Paris any longer than the 27th, but he apparently persuaded them to wait. It is believed that Soustelle wanted de Gaulle to come to power by constitutional means if possible for the political advantages this course offered, rather than by a *coup d'état*, and he also lent his weight to persuade the generals and impatient colonels to hold their hand.

On the 25th, the All Algerian Committee of Public Safety announced that it would hand over its powers to General de Gaulle and to no one else, which seemed to rather force the issue for Pflimlin, who had a secret meeting with de Gaulle the next day. On the 27th, de Gaulle issued a statement saying that he 'had begun normal processes to re-establish Republican Government'. This caused massive demonstrations in Paris, organized by the Communists, as a protest. Pflimlin resigned the same day, but President Coty asked him to continue temporarily as a caretaker Prime Minister, which he agreed to do.

The acute suspense continued. Most now hoped that it would be possible for General de Gaulle to take over the government by peaceful means, as by the French constitution it was not essential that the Prime Minister be a member of the National Assembly. On the 29th, when there was still no overt sign of a satisfactory solution, President Coty said he would resign unless the National Assembly accepted de Gaulle as leader, and there was a general sigh of relief in most quarters the next day (30th), when de Gaulle agreed to form a Government. On 1st June he became Prime Minister of France, but one condition of his acceptance was that he be given full powers for a period of six months.

Having been confirmed as Prime Minister, one of de Gaulle's first acts, after persuading the National Assembly to authorize him to draw up a new constitution for the country, was to send it into recess for four months. On his first day in office he lifted the censorship ban. His first Cabinet was conservative, if not to say cautious, and contained no Algerian insurrection personalities. This omission was criticized by Delbecque, who had done so much to help de Gaulle return to power, while the Europeans in Algeria were disappointed that Soustelle had not been included.

De Gaulle visited Algeria in the second week in June, where

he was given a tremendous reception, especially by the Europeans, who expected big things from him in return for their part in bringing him back to power. De Gaulle was polite, unyielding and non-committal. He brought Generals Salan and Massu to heel, and persuaded them to curb the hotheads. The Europeans tried to pressure him into appointing Soustelle as Resident Minister, but he would not agree. Before leaving the country, de Gaulle drily warned the All Algerian Committee of Public Safety not to exceed its functions. His brief visit acted like a cold shower on the heated emotions of the Europeans and the Army in Algeria. On 16th June, de Gaulle formally appointed General Salan the Delegate-General of the French Government in Algeria.

Other measures de Gaulle put into effect included reducing the budget of the 5th Bureau, the army psychological warfare branch, thus depriving the Army of much of its political power and means. General Ely was recalled as Chief of Staff of the Armed Forces, and given the task of scattering the army plotters who over the next weeks and months were quietly, in twos and threes, posted from Algeria to France, Germany or elsewhere.

One by one, key administrative posts in Algeria were filled with hand-picked civilians and army officers, and the European Ultras gradually found themselves out-manœuvred and losing power. Soustelle was recalled to France, almost by a trick, where he was kept waiting. It was not until 7th July that de Gaulle appointed him Minister of Information. Delbecque also returned to France, regretting his outspoken criticism of his leader, to be treated coolly.

De Gaulle paid his second visit to Algeria during the first week of July. As he was particularly anxious about feeling in the Army, this was mainly to inspect army units, test the political atmosphere and to put over his own personality. He gathered groups of officers around him and spoke to them at every unit and post he went to. To the Europeans he showed an almost open indifference, presenting them with what might be interpreted as a challenge by taking with him on the visit the unpopular Mollet, who two years earlier had been pelted with tomatoes by European Ultras. He also refused to receive a deputation from the All Algerian Committee of Public Safety, again issuing a barely veiled warning. De Gaulle also made efforts to woo the Muslims, speaking to groups of them whenever he could. He pledged an extra $35 million to be added to the Algerian budget to be spent on development, and also announced that he planned to set up electoral lists, establish a single electoral college of Algeria and give the vote to women.

This second visit left no doubt in anyone's mind that he was not going to be under anyone's influence, nor was he going to react to pressures from any one group or faction. De Gaulle was going his own way. He made vague pronouncements on Algeria, and would not endorse the policy of Muslim and European integration as put forward by the 5th Bureau of the Army in the insurrection period.

Gradually the emphasis on 'French Algeria' was lessened, and integration of Muslims and Europeans was heard of with rapidly decreasing frequency. Army officers were instructed to devote more attention to the war and less to playing politics, and indirect pressure was applied to encourage them to this end. The authority of commanding officers to provide guidance on what their men should write home about Algeria was removed. Outwardly submissive, the Europeans, especially the Ultras, seethed with discontent and disappointment at de Gaulle's attitude, while on the other hand the FLN heaved sighs of relief. It had nearly lost its political platform.

Later, in a referendum, held in September 1958, 80 per cent of the French people voted in favour of General de Gaulle's new constitution, and at the November elections he was returned as Prime Minister, when Communist representation in the National Assembly was reduced from 145 seats down to only 10. Presidential elections took place on 21st December, and resulted in de Gaulle being elected to that office, which he assumed on 8th January 1959, with more power than his predecessor, President Coty.

Swept into power by events in which he was in no way

directly responsible, once in high office, General de Gaulle disregarded the interests of the Europeans in Algeria, the people who had played a major part in putting him where he was. Deserted by Soustelle and Delbecque, the Europeans felt bewildered and embittered. The FLN was quite pleased. De Gaulle's policy was now to separate the Europeans from the Army, and to separate the Army from politics. But there was strong resistance and resentment, and he had to move warily.

CHAPTER 6

Fourth Year of the War

1958

During the early part of the fourth year of the war the ALN engaged French troops in a series of battles in the region of the Tunisian frontier, in which it suffered great losses, causing it to revert to smaller fighting formations and guerilla tactics.

Several ALN battalions, and even on occasions regiments of two or more battalions, came into violent contact with French troops when attempting to cross the frontier between Algeria and Tunisia. The ALN was working up for a spring offensive and wanted to filter large numbers of troops from the training camps in Tunisia into Algeria. It also wanted to send many of the unarmed and untrained Moussebilines and Fidayines into Tunisia for training and to be armed. The ALN had evolved a technique, a desperate one, for cutting the electrified wire of the Morice Line. Insurgent fighters approached it at one point from both sides to simultaneously cut through the wire strands with wire-cutters insulated to take up to 12,000 volts. This, of course, gave immediate warning to the nearest French detachment manning that particular sector, which rushed to the scene in both helicopters and vehicles. Inevitably, there was a fierce clash which ended with many ALN dead, for usually comparatively light French losses. The insurgents had only minutes to get through the cut wire, but the need to break across the frontier was so urgent that such dangerous methods had to be adopted. Whenever possible, bangalore torpedoes were also used, but this technique was never really developed, partly because of shortage of bangalore torpedoes and partly because owing to the width and construction of the Morice Line they were often only partially effective.

On 4th January 1958 a band of ALN recruits being escorted into Tunisia for training was waylaid near Tebessa, French troops killing 81 of them and capturing another 41. A week later, on the 10th, another ALN group returning from training in Tunisia was virtually wiped out when 116 insurgents were killed and 31 captured.

In the Guelma area, between 27th January and 5th February, 221 insurgents were killed, and between 9th and 11th February, 64 more were killed in a fight with the French. In the second half of the month, in a series of major clashes in the vicinity of Guelma and Duvivier (about 30 miles south of Bône), over 500 ALN fighters were killed between the 14th and 26th. On the 27th, an ALN battalion, crossing the frontier near El-Ma-El-Aboid, was detected by radar and brought to battle in the Nementcha Mountains, when 110 insurgents were killed.

Heavy snowfalls in the early part of March restricted activity, but on the 6th, 30 uniformed insurgents were killed in a clash near Duvivier, and on the 8th another 26 were killed in the Nementcha Mountains, after having entered Algeria by the southern route. Paratroop attacks on the ALN in the area between Bône and Duvivier on the 18th, resulted in 122 insurgents killed, for the loss of 25 French troops. On the 29th, an ALN battalion, 450 strong, was attacked when breaking through the Morice Line, and 120 insurgent fighters were killed in the clash.

These attempts, many almost suicidal, to break through the electrified Morice Line, caused the French to take additional measures, and they created an artificial 'No Man's Land' along the Tunisian frontier on the Algerian side, varying in width from 6 to 30 miles, where patrolling and static French troops shot on sight anything that moved. To clear this area some 70,000 Algerians were forcibly moved away into regroupment camps. This further restricted ALN units crossing the borders, but despite heavy casualties they continued with the same tactics of literally charging their way through with their heads down. As the ALN policy remained to have units of battalion size, or larger, these tactics caused several minor mutinies by insurgents who refused to face such odds.

Apart from the 'frontier battles', in Kabylie there had been heavy fighting during the first two months of the year, and French official sources estimated, for example, that between 27th January and 20th February, the ALN suffered 2,151 killed and 333 wounded or taken prisoner.[1] Another bad period for the ALN, also in the Kabylie area, was from 23rd to 29th March, when 806 uniformed insurgent fighters were killed and another 85 taken prisoner.

April was also a bad time for the insurgents, and during the first fortnight or so of this month 11 ALN Moujahidines, uniformed fighters, were killed just to the west of Bir-El-Ater, another 98 in two actions in the Souk-Ahras area, and a further 150 in the Nementcha Mountains.

The largest battle of the whole war took place between 28th April and 3rd May, when an ALN regiment, numbering nearly 1,000 fighters, tried to bulldoze its way through the Morice Line near Souk-Ahras. In the first two days, 436 insurgents were killed and 100 captured, as well as quantities of arms and ammunition seized. On a renewal of the fighting after a brief lull, another 93 insurgents were killed, after which about 250 of the survivors retreated back into Tunisia, and the remainder escaped into the hills. The cost to the French in this six days' hard fighting was 38 killed and 35 wounded.

Similar engagements in the same area during May cost the ALN at least 169 killed. During the following month, June, the pace slackened as the ALN units were less keen to break through the Morice Line and face the French small-arms fire, but nevertheless several attempts were still made. One of the last of the large-scale attempts to crash forcibly through this formidable barrier, the whole series of which came to be known as the 'Battle of the Frontier', occurred on 26th June near Tebessa, when a battalion about 300 strong clashed violently with French

---

[1] In February 1958, French casualties in Algeria amounted to 360 killed and 700 wounded (as against 203 killed in February 1957). No other breakdown figures were issued.

troops. Forty-six insurgents were killed and 64 captured, while the remainder hastily withdrew into Tunisia. On the same day, about 30 recruits attempting to get into Tunisia were killed by French troops near Bir-El-Ater.

Despite scornful FLN propaganda, the electrified barrier, the Morice Line, effectively kept ALN units, amounting to about 10,000 armed and uniformed soldiers in 10 or 12 battalions, out of Algeria, although it took some 30,000 French troops to accomplish this. This confinement was maintained right until the end of the war, during which time the major part of the ALN was helplessly held back from battle. In the many head-on clashes with the French Army in the early months of 1958, the ALN, in battalion-sized units, had come off a poor second best. The French had better and more powerful arms, mobility and aircraft, against which the insurgents could only fight back with infantry weapons.

French estimates, at the beginning of the year, 1958, credit the ALN with a strength of about 30,000 regular fighters, that is Moujahidines, of whom only about 15,000 were operating inside Algeria at any one time, and about 30,000 para-military fighters, or Moussebilines, most of whom were in Algeria. The ALN at this time claimed to have at least a fighting strength of 100,000, but this obviously included the Fidayines, the village militia, and the OPA, the political and supporting organization. During the first seven months of the year, the French estimated that the ALN lost in battle 23,534 insurgents killed or captured.[1] The strength of the ALN remained fairly constant, as recruits were forthcoming[2] more readily, being now attracted by the glamour of fighting a nationalist war against a Colonial Power. During 1958, numbers of Moussebilines and Fidayines, as they were recruited, were sent as quickly as possible out of the country to the Eastern or Western Bases to be armed and

[1] French figures later released showed the ALN casualties, during the Battle of the Frontier, to be:

February 1958	—	3,401 killed and 529 captured
March 1958	—	3,132 killed and 715 captured
April 1958	—	3,728 killed and 756 captured.

[2] There were about 5 million Algerian Muslims under 20 years of age.

trained. Another reason for doing this was to prevent them being caught up in the wholesale removal of sections of the population that was just getting under way, when they would most probably be lost to the ALN.

Apart from the resultant heavy casualties, it was brought home to the ALN higher command that the field tactics were all wrong, and that it had been a mistake to try and match punch for punch with the French Army and to operate in battalion-sized formations at this stage of development. The decision to reverse this was taken, and commencing in June, the ALN battalions were broken up. The company, or 'katiba', was to be the basic fighting unit in the future. The katibas were to concentrate on offensive guerilla activity and not to fight any positional battles against equal, or even slightly smaller French units. In other words, according to the insurgent warfare blueprint, the ALN had jumped from the guerilla warfare stage right into the final conventional one — or at least had tried to do so.

The ALN set up two separate general staffs in Algeria, one under Mohammed Said, to organize and instigate operations in the eastern part of the country, and the other under Aimirouche Ait Hamouda, who had become the commander of Wilaya II, to control the fighting in the western part.

Apart from the regions affected directly by the Battle of the Frontier, the ALN elsewhere had also been working with battalion-sized units wherever it could, but these had been mainly content to use hit-and-run tactics, and to avoid battle whenever possible. Whenever these guerilla tactics were practised they were often successful, and French patrols were ambushed and small French posts raided for arms.

Of the larger clashes in which the ALN suffered notable casualties, one can be mentioned which took place near Saida on 7th January (1958), when 80 insurgents were killed, another, a three-day battle, from the 5th to 8th March, south of Algiers, resulted in 51 insurgents killed and 23 wounded (the French lost 17 killed), and on the 16th, an ALN convoy was attacked in the Collo Peninsula area, when 80 insurgents were killed.

On 23rd May, 53 insurgents were killed near Ain Sefra, and on the 27th, another 37 were killed south of Saida. In a four-day battle beginning on 28th May, near Molière in Ouarsenis, 163 insurgents were killed and 31 captured, while on 4th June, another 52 were killed in the Churchell area, on the coast to the west of Algiers. And so on. All of which indicated to the ALN commanders that it would be wiser to revert to smaller units and to avoid head-on clashes until the ALN was better armed and trained, more ALN formations had been filtered in from Tunisia, and the French Army was correspondingly frustrated, weakened and dispersed. The system of quadrillage had enabled the French to stem the insurrection by mid-1958, and so bring about a favourable stalemate.

An additional reason for abandoning battalion-sized attack tactics was that ALN morale had taken a beating, and in many cases was breaking, or near to breaking point. In several instances it had actually broken, and the units disintegrated, not always under the stress of battle conditions. Another period of gentle blooding for the newly trained recruits, who formed up to 80 per cent of the uniformed fighters, the Moujahidines, was essential to condition them for future battles.

At a conference held at Tangiers in May 1958, the FLN wanted to form a Government-in-Exile, but both Tunisia and Morocco objected, partly because they did not wish to forfeit the French assistance and benefits they were receiving to help develop their newly independent countries, and partly because they were not sure that the French Army could be restrained from taking reprisals over their borders if they supported such a move. Disappointed, Ferhat Abbas tried again to win support for his idea at the Second African Conference, held in Tunis in June, but with no more success, President Bourguiba flatly refusing to back any FLN Government-in-Exile.

Receiving no support from either Tunisia or Morocco, the FLN turned towards Nasser of Egypt, and found more encouragement. General de Gaulle's coolness to the European demands may have influenced the FLN into taking a bolder course. On 16th September 1958, the FLN announced that it had formed a 'Free Algerian Government-in-Exile' in Cairo, and this was immediately recognized by Arab countries, including Tunisia and Morocco (who could do no other in the face of a *fait accompli*), and Pakistan and Red China. On the 23rd, it was recognized by Indonesia, and other recognitions followed at intervals. It is extremely probable that the formation of this Government-in-Exile was a calculated counter-measure to de Gaulle's expected referendum victory.

The first Prime Minister of the Free Algerian Government-in-Exile (or Provisional Algerian Government, as it came to be known) was Ferhat Abbas, with Belkacem Krim as a Vice-Prime Minister and Minister of the Armed Forces, and Ben Bella as the other Vice-Prime Minister. Lamine-Debaghine became Minister of Foreign Affairs. Of the 14 members of the Government, only two had Arabic as their first language, the remainder were happier conversing and writing in French. The French insisted that the Provisional Algerian Government sought to impose itself on the people of Algeria, had no mandate from them, and the ministers little in common with the average Algerian Muslim peasant.

The Arab League made financial contributions to the Provisional Algerian Government's war chest, which amounted to about £12 million in 1958, of which the United Arab Republic (Egypt) provided about 75 per cent. Funds began to arrive from Red China, and extended credits had been granted by some Iron Curtain and certain Western countries for some time for the purchase of arms. Generally for the first four years of the war the insurgents had to rely largely upon their own efforts.

The struggle between the FLN and the MNA continued, both politically and militarily. In Algeria, the MNA fought a losing battle, but in France they were more evenly matched. The main group of armed MNA fighters in Algeria, the National Army of the Algerian People, was still under the leadership of Mohammed Bellounis, who had come to an arrangement with the French, but elements of it increasingly fell under ALN influence and began to defect. In April (1958) one group of about 1,000 went over to the ALN, and another group flatly refused to withdraw from the Laghouat area when ordered to do so by the French. On 1st May, French troops were sent to enforce this order, and in the ensuing battle 81 MNA uniformed fighters were killed.

Bellounis turned against the French after General de Gaulle came to power, and on 16th June, announced that he would henceforth fight for the independence of Algeria. As his army in the mountains and countryside faded away, he concentrated upon urban terrorism, especially against FLN sympathizers. The ALN terrorist organization in Algiers had been rooted out by General Massu, but many MNA members had remained at large underground. These were reorganized and began a spate of assassinations, carried out by special squads, which were claimed to be 'death sentences'. This in turn sparked off a revival of ALN underground terrorists, who again became active in the city against the Muslim population.

Mohammed Bellounis was killed on 14th July, in a clash with French troops near Bou Saada. Shortly afterwards, the bodies of over 500 Muslims were discovered, murdered, it is thought, on his instructions as a reprisal for the Melouza Massacre (of May 1957), when the male inhabitants of the village of Melouza had been killed by the ALN because the village had sought MNA protection.

The other turncoat operating with the French in the Orléansville area, Belhadj Djilal, was murdered by his own followers on 29th April, when some 850 of his men joined the ALN *en bloc*.

On General de Gaulle's orders the French Army in Algeria had to make cease-fire contacts with the ALN. The French also continued the tactics of encouraging desertion and counter-insurgency with varying degrees of success. Both these methods hit the insurgents hard where it hurt most, and they took the most bitter reprisals on any suspected of collaborating with, or going over to, the French side. For example, on 22nd September French soldiers discovered some 400 Muslims dead in the Akfadou Forest in Kabylie, alleged to have been killed (in June) by Aimirouche Ait Hamouda, the Wilaya Commander, when he unearthed a plot against himself and discovered that a section of his force was planning to desert to the French. Many of the corpses were partially burnt or mutilated, and some had the Cross of Lorraine, the symbol associated with General de Gaulle, marked by knife slashes on the backs. On the other hand, Aimirouche Ait Hamouda had released several European prisoners who had been kidnapped by his men.

The French had some success in suborning ALN rank and file at times, and persuaded many to change sides, or, when captured, to return to their former units as French intelligence agents. However, all such attempts were not successful, and one of the largest failures was that of Si Azzedine, the second-in-command of Wilaya IV, who agreed, after being wounded and captured by the French in November 1958, to return to his Wilaya to negotiate for a surrender. He published a declaration saying that the return to power of General de Gaulle made a nonsense of the Algerian rebellion, and given a safe conduct pass, was able to go freely from one side to the other. He fed false information to the French, and also used a temporary local cease-fire to enable a convoy of supplies and equipment to reach ALN units in his Wilaya. The FLN often boasted about this stratagem but in reality it was one of their few successes in this field. Mostly, ALN defectors carried out their tasks of counter-insurgency reasonably effectively.

On the other hand, the ALN had some success also in persuading Algerian Muslims serving in the French Army, or as auxiliaries, in Algeria to desert with their arms if possible. General Salan, the Commander-in-Chief of the Army in Algeria, concentrated upon increasing the numbers of the Algerian Muslims in the French Army and the Harkis. One notable occasion was on 10th April, when 10 Muslim officers deserted to the ALN. Precise figures of Muslim deserters from the French services were not released by the French, but later it was said[1] that the number of Muslim deserters had declined from 366 in

[1] On 12th November 1958, by the Minister of the Armed Forces. These were obviously carefully selected sets of figures. Later, on 10th November 1959, General de Gaulle gave a figure of 1·4 per 1,000 per month as Muslim deserters from the French forces.

March 1956 to only 80 in October 1958. It was said at the time that ALN fighters coming over to the French side had risen from one in March 1956, to an average of 300 in July and August 1958.

In France, gang terrorism and warfare between the Muslim underground organizations rose to its height in 1958, when some 902 Algerian Muslims were killed, the numbers of dead being almost equally divided between the FLN and the MNA. Ferhat Abbas admitted at a press interview that his Government had reluctantly given the FLN subversive organization in France permission to increase terrorism in September 1958, but restricting such attacks to military targets and economic ones of military importance. He said that some of his advisers had urged that this permission be given much earlier.

Removing sections of the population to enable the French Army to fight more freely and to prevent people passing intelligence, and giving support, to the insurgents continued, and it was stated that there were 364,000 people in regroupment centres in December 1957, and this figure rose to 485,000 by August the following year. Many areas were declared to be 'Forbidden Zones' for strategical or security reasons and forcibly cleared of people. Regroupment centres placed the people in them under direct military control and protection.

The Safeguard Commission, which had remained inactive since submitting its first report (published in December 1957), was revived by General de Gaulle. He gave it greater powers and also authority to investigate in Metropolitan France, but its findings were not to be made public.

The refugee problem became acute as Algerian Muslims fled into Tunisia and Morocco to escape being caught up in regroupment schemes, to avoid French internment or punishment for insurgent activities, or under the urging of the FLN and the ALN. By December 1957, there were, according to Red Cross estimates, about 60,000 Algerian refugees in Tunisia and about 40,000 in Morocco. In January 1958, America agreed to supply food to Tunisia for 60,000 Algerian refugees for three months. By November that year, the Moroccan delegate to the

UN claimed that there were 70,000 Algerian Muslim refugees in Morocco and another 130,000 in Tunisia. These figures may have been largely correct.

The FLN protested against death sentences carried out by the French on captured insurgents (to whom the French refused to give the status of prisoners of war), claiming that, for example, between 11th January and 4th March (1958), 11 ALN soldiers had been guillotined and 11 more sentenced to death. Executions by the French continued, and during April 12 more captured insurgents were guillotined.

On 9th May, the FLN announced that in reprisal the ALN had executed three captured French soldiers (on 24th April).[1] On 9th July, a captured French officer was executed on the orders of Aimirouche Ait Hamouda. The French had refused to exchange him for FLN prisoners. On 20th October, the four French soldiers who had been captured near Sakiet (on 11th January 1958) were handed over by the FLN to Red Cross officials in Tunis. A fortnight later, General Salan ordered the release of 10 ALN prisoners as a return gesture. It was also officially announced on 21st October that over 14,000 Algerian Muslims had been released from internment since 13th May.

During the referendum campaign in Algeria in September, the 5th Bureau of the Army prompted, encouraged and urged the whole army to put out propaganda for de Gaulle. Over three million pamphlets were distributed, and over half a million posters affixed, as well as innumerable 'Ouis' painted on buildings and walls. French soldiers were encouraged to tell the Muslims that a vote of 'Non' amounted to a vote for Communism, and General Salan told the people that the Mediterranean crosses France as the Seine crosses Paris. Army vehicles carried Muslim voters to the polls, and also toured the streets with loud-speakers urging everyone to come out and vote.

The ALN threatened Muslims, warning that the roads to the polling booths would be mined, ordering them to stay at home; if they could not they were instructed to leave their registration

---

[1] The event that had done much to spark the European insurrection in Algiers that resulted in General de Gaulle being returned to power.

cards at home, or to vote 'Non'. Despite the threats and pressure, the Algerian Muslims turned out to vote for de Gaulle in unexpected strength.

Following General de Gaulle's success in the referendum, measures began to be put into effect in Algeria to further decentralize administration, and to give the Muslims a larger hand in it. This caused the Europeans, already sulky and suspicious of de Gaulle's intentions, to become more discontented and non-co-operative. Acts of terrorism and violence by Ultras began to occur and to increase steadily in number. On 3rd October, General de Gaulle announced a Five-Year Plan for Algeria, sometimes known as the Constantine Plan, the objects of which were to improve agriculture, industrial development, Muslim education and to bring an increased number of Muslims into the government service. This displeased the Europeans, and on the 15th, the All Algerian Committee of Public Safety, which had remained in being, called for a general strike in protest. It was persuaded not to take this course by General Salan.

De Gaulle went further, forbidding military officers to stand for the forthcoming local elections in Algeria, and ordering them to retire from politics at once. On 14th October, General Massu and other army officers on the All Algerian Committee of Public Safety resigned, and this example was followed elsewhere in the country where there were Committees of Public Safety. General de Gaulle had taken another firm step towards reducing the political power of the Army in Algeria.

Local elections were held in Algeria on 30th November, when 67 per cent of the electorate voted. There was only one attack on a polling station, in which six insurgents were killed, but generally this time the ALN had far more success with their threats and intimidation campaign in persuading the Muslims to stay at home.

On 23rd October, General de Gaulle gave his first press conference since taking office. He offered an amnesty to all insurgents who surrendered, and invited the FLN to send representatives to Paris under a safe-conduct pass to negotiate a cease-fire. This became known as his offer of the 'Peace of the Brave'.[1] The French Army in Algeria, and the 5th Bureau in particular, had so far continued with a propaganda policy of integrating European and Muslim in a French Algeria. Now this was dropped suddenly and the Army went all out to persuade the Muslims to accept the Peace of the Brave. On the 25th, the FLN firmly rejected General de Gaulle's demand for an unconditional surrender, but offered to open negotiations in a neutral country. De Gaulle did not respond to this for the time being.

The defeat of the ALN in the Battle of the Frontier caused not only a change in ALN strategy and tactics, but also gave an impetus for munitions and supplies to be channelled to Morocco, thus giving an added importance to the Western Base. Fewer attempts were made to breach the Morice Line, but instead the longer way round to the south to avoid it was used, both to send recruits into Tunisia to train and to import arms and equipment, most of which were carried by returning recruits or brought in on camels. This route was quite dangerous owing to the French having both radar warning systems and aircraft surveillance. The breaking up of the ALN battalions, started in June, took weeks to carry into effect, and although the official ALN strategy became one of guerilla warfare, there were still occasionally large-scale clashes, either because local commanders had not got around to reducing the size of their units into katibas, or companies, or were reluctant to do so, or because French sweeps managed at times to corner large numbers of insurgents.

Generally there were numerous small actions of various types, such as ambushes, over the length and breadth of the country for the second part of 1958, producing both ALN and French casualties, but there were exceptions. For instance, on 6th July 75 insurgents were killed near Medea, on the 28th another 117

---

[1] General de Gaulle also said at the press conference that since November 1954, 7,200 French soldiers and 77,000 insurgents had been killed in the fighting, and that 1,500 European civilians and over 10,000 Muslims had lost their lives as a result of the war.

were killed in the Bou Saada area, on the 30th 55 were killed in the Djurdjura Mountains, and on 1st August 69 more were killed in the Bou Saada area. On 28th August a French troop train was mined between Batna and Biskra, when 12 French soldiers were killed and 20 more injured.

During the second half of September, French forces in Algeria had been on the defensive to protect the electorate during the referendum for the new constitution. October saw a series of French operations against the ALN in the Saida Mountains and Kabylie, during which 224 insurgents were killed and a large encampment and store base were discovered and destroyed. In the same month a combined ground and air sweep killed 139 insurgents between Tlemcen and Tiaret. There was a revival of ALN activity in the Sahara in the summer, and on 20th August 15 insurgents were killed near Colomb Béchar, but on 19th September 16 French soldiers were killed in ambush in the same district. A somewhat similar pattern continued until the end of the year.

All in all, it could be said that 1958 was a bad year for the ALN fighting in Algeria. In January 1959, the Provisional Algerian Government admitted that it saw no prospect of peace in Algeria, but that it was prepared to continue the war for many years. The Provisional Algerian Government decided to transfer its headquarters to Rabat, in Morocco. This was thought to be a sign of disappointment at lack of expected generous support for the UAR and the Arab League.

CHAPTER 7

The Challe Plan

1959

During 1959, French Army strategy underwent a change in Algeria, being re-orientated by a new Commander-in-Chief. This began on 15th December (1958), when General de Gaulle made further changes in senior appointments in Algeria. He removed General Salan to a specially created post in France, as Inspector-General of National Defence.[1] Salan's former duties were divided between Paul Delouvrier, who was appointed Delegate-General, assuming supreme civil authority, and General Maurice Challe, an air force officer, who was appointed Commander-in-Chief of all the French forces in Algeria.

The quadrillage system employed by the French Army to counter ALN insurgency tactics was reasonably successful in blanketing free movement and curbing infiltration into population centres, but its main drawback was that it required so many troops to sit in the cities, towns and large villages, that few were left to go out and destroy ALN units in the mountains and countryside. This mobile force, made up of units of French volunteers, paratroops and Foreign Legionnaires, seldom exceeded 15,000, which was roughly the same strength as the ALN could muster inside Algeria for active operations. Reviewing the situation from a military point of view, General Challe instituted several changes. Already about 1,500 French officers had been transferred from Algeria; and, purged of extremists

---

[1] General Salan was later appointed Military Governor of Paris, a sinecure, and then retired in June 1960 on reaching the age limit.

with strong political views and sympathies, the Army was becoming a more efficient, cohesive fighting force.

General Challe realized that one of the most important priorities was to keep the Tunisian and Moroccan frontiers strongly guarded, so that the growing number of ALN units being formed and trained in those two countries would be prevented from entering Algeria. Another important priority was to destroy the regular ALN elements operating inside Algeria. The next part of what came to be known as the 'Challe Plan' was to root out the OPA, the insurgent political and administrative organization which supported the ALN in the field and enabled it to gain and keep a hold over the minds and loyalties of the majority of the Muslims. The other priority was to substitute a French-Algerian society as an ideal in place of the FLN notion of Algerian independence.

While basically retaining the quadrillage system, General Challe reduced the number of French troops statically employed, and correspondingly increased the strength of the mobile reserve for use against areas where the ALN had become firmly ensconced and had established small bases. He also reformed certain Algerian-Muslim units and gave them a 'sharpshooter' role. General Challe also instituted the 'Commandos de Chasse', units of about 100 soldiers, both French and Muslim. Each commando was required to track down a particular katiba, the now basic regular ALN field unit, and to constantly supply information by radio about its movements so that larger mobile French forces could be brought against it at an opportune time and place.

Before an offensive was launched the area against which it was directed would be isolated by surrounding it with a 'pacified zone', too wide to be crossed in a single night by insurgent units. These tactics were used with good effect during 1959 in a series of sweeps and offensives against the ALN in mountainous areas, getting off to a good start when, between the 6th and 8th of January, French forces operating in the mountains just to the south-west of Tizi-Ouzou, in Kabylie, killed over 300 insurgents for the loss of 22 French paratroops.

THE CHALLE PLAN

Beginning in February, French military operations were mounted against the ALN in the Ouarsenis, especially in the Frenda Mountains and near Saida. These lasted until the end of April when it was officially given out that the Ouarsenis was cleared of insurgents. More military posts were set up, administrative and social services were installed, and many miles of mountain tracks were made motorable. During these operations over 1,600 insurgents were killed, 460 were captured and large stocks of ammunition and other stores were seized. The OPA, the political and administrative underground organization, was broken up and over 1,100 arrests made.

Between the 5th and 11th of March, a similar operation in the region of Tizi-Ouzou resulted in 142 insurgents killed. On the 22nd, an ALN group, about 150 strong, crossed into Algeria from Tunisia and gave itself up to the French.

A morale booster for the French, and a corresponding dampener for the ALN, occurred on 28th March in a fight in Kabylie near Bou Saada, when two Wilaya commanders were killed. One was the by now famous Aimirouche Ait Hamouda, the commander of Wilaya III and the Chief of Staff of the ALN in western Algeria, and considered by the French to be the best of the ALN field commanders. In command of the Kabylie Wilaya since 1957, he had made it into a formidable stronghold. The other was Si Haoues, the commander of Wilaya IV.

There were occasional attempts to break through the Morice Line from Tunisia, and on 13th February two ALN katibas trying to cross the frontier this way lost 175 killed or captured near Tebessa in a fight with French troops, for the loss of only three French soldiers. In April and May numbers of ALN fighters in Tunisia were reported to be asking to be interned by the Tunisian authorities to avoid being sent into action against the Morice Line. Attacks against the Morice Line and attempts to break through it led General Challe to erect a second mined and electrified barbed wire entanglement along the Tunisian frontier. This was a further obstacle to hamper the ALN, forcing all recruits passing between Tunisia and Algeria to go round by the long route south, which both took a long time and was hazardous owing to radar detection devices and French aircraft patrols. The only alternative was to send recruits for training to Morocco, where there were fewer facilities, and also similar barriers along parts of the frontier.

By summer the Challe Plan began really to get into its stride, and a large operation took place between the 9th and 20th of July in the Hodna Mountains, which had been used as a connecting link by the insurgents between the Aures and the Kabylie Mountains. The area was surrounded by several thousand troops, who closed steadily inwards, killing or capturing ALN fighters as they penetrated this small insurgent stronghold, held, at an estimate, by about 4,500 ALN fighters. At times there was hard fighting by cornered ALN soldiers, and 404 were killed and 138 taken prisoner, for the loss of 46 French troops killed and 69 wounded. Also, 141 members of the OPA were arrested. Extensive underground installations with store-rooms, medical centres, and stocks of ammunition, food and clothing were discovered and destroyed. New French military and administrative posts, as well as social services, were established in the Hodna Mountains area.

General Challe personally took command of a prolonged operation in Grand Kabylie, in the area between Tizi-Ouzou and Bougie, which had been a strong and troublesome ALN sector since the beginning of the war. This was known as Operation 'Binoculars'. With a population of perhaps 900,000, mostly in scattered villages perched on mountain-sides, this had been a valuable ALN recruiting ground. The main objects of the operation were to eliminate ALN radio installations in the area and to root out the OPA, which was responsible for recruiting both for the ALN field force and for terrorist activities in Algiers and other cities. About 20,000 French troops were employed, and in the initial stages marines were landed on the coast and paratroops dropped at vital points inland. Starting on 22nd July, this operation continued until the last days of October, when it was announced that 3,746 insurgents had been killed, captured or wounded. Under this great pressure the ALN katibas, each of about 100 men, had to split into smaller sections of between 10 and 20 to try and escape. The ALN fighters were driven to take refuge in the many mountain caves in the area.

Similar, but smaller, French operations took place in the Soummam Valley, Kabylie, in August and again in October. A FLN spokesman admitted that the ALN was at times losing about 500 men a day during this period. If this was so, the silent desertion figure must have been much higher than was realized.

Keeping up the same unrelenting pressure and using the same strategy and tactics, General Challe next launched two more large operations, both on the same day, 1st November. One, known as Operation 'Turquoise', was to clear the area to the north of Constantine, which included the Djidjelli and Mila sectors. The other, known as Operation 'Emerald', was to clear the Collo Peninsula and the Philippeville and Bône sectors. In both areas the ALN had troop concentrations and many installations, as well as a strong supporting OPA. About 22,000 French troops of all sorts were employed, and when these two massive operations ran down by the end of March (1960), it was claimed that over 2,500 insurgents had been killed, wounded or captured. About 80,000 people had been forcibly removed to regroupment centres to clear terrain so that the troops could operate more freely against the insurgents. New military and administrative posts were established and more miles of roadway constructed.

When General Challe left Algeria (22nd April 1960), in a farewell Order of the Day he claimed that during his tour of command over half the ALN forces in the country had been either killed or captured, meaning that about 40 of the probable 80 katibas operating inside Algeria had been destroyed, that the remaining units had been forced to reduce their size or disperse, that acts of terrorism had also fallen by half, and that the ALN in Algeria had been increasingly cut off from external aid and support. Some critics doubted these claims, being of the view that General Challe's massive sweeps had merely caused the ALN troops to withdraw in typical guerilla-like avoidance tactics, and that the OPA, which had been a main target, had merely been forced underground. While there may have been some substance in the critics' remarks, the general overall assessment must be that General Challe's claims were largely correct. Ferhat Abbas was forced to admit that the position was that he could see no 'military solution' to the FLN problem of gaining complete independence. The broken OPA was succeeded by the ORU (Organisation Rurale et Urbaine) which concentrated on political duties and fund collecting.

The ALN had been forced to revert further back into the guerilla stage of the insurgent blue-print, and it could be said that it had been completely forced out of the protracted one. In two years, largely as a result of the Challe Plan, the ALN had been compelled to scale down from battalion to section actions. Even so, although morale was badly shaken, there was still fight left in the hard core of the ALN in the field in Algeria.

The FLN put on a bold front, boasting that it had over 100,000 men under arms, and that it could keep up the same pace indefinitely, but it was probable that the ALN was reduced to about 30,000 fighters in all, of whom less than 15,000 were inside Algeria. This latter figure now probably included most of the Moussebilines and Fidayines who had been rapidly absorbed into the regular ALN element, the Moujahidines, to replace casualties, as fewer and fewer reinforcements managed to get back into Algeria from either Tunisia or Morocco owing to the strong French frontier measures.

General Challe's assertion that terrorism had decreased was contradicted by the Europeans, as well as the ALN. The first large bomb explosion since 2nd August 1957 occurred in Algiers on 18th April 1959, and this coincided with similar bomb outrages in Constantine and other Algerian cities, mainly as a demonstration against municipal elections. There were other bomb explosions in Algiers with loss of life on 25th September, 11th October and 24th December, which helped to substantiate the Europeans' insistence that terrorism was on the increase. This was eventually denied by Delouvrier, the Delegate-

General, who gave out official figures of civilian casualties caused by terrorists.[1] Forcible removal of large sections of the population had been put into practice in a big way during 1958, especially in the eastern frontier areas, to allow French troops a free hand to fight, to remove potential sources of ALN supply, intelligence and support, and to inhibit the subversive activities of the OPA agents. By March 1959, numbers in regroupment centres exceeded one million, when, owing to criticism of this policy in Metropolitan France, Delouvrier, the Delegate-General, ordered that no more should be moved into these centres unless he gave special permission. However, this practice had to continue under the Challe Plan but more circumspectly. The Challe Plan required a pacified zone to surround any area marked out for future operations, and this meant removing the population. This policy not only caused thousands to be uprooted, but also caused many Muslims to flock to the cities and towns to avoid being caught up and put into a regroupment centre; as a result they simply swelled the depressed slum populations.

Conditions in the various regroupment centres varied: some were good, but others gave rise to alarming rumours of overcrowding and insanitary conditions. In some, psychological warfare methods were practised by the Army's 5th Bureau. FLN propaganda made much capital out of the regroupment centres.

Conditions were more severe and almost oppressive in the internment camps, which contained arrested political prisoners and ALN personnel captured in battle. As a gesture, General de Gaulle had released about 1,000 internees on 31st October 1958, when he made his appeal for the Peace of the Brave. On 13th January 1959 he announced an amnesty for insurgent fighters, when he commuted about 180 capital sentences and

[1] These were:

June	1958	— 259 civilians killed, 308 wounded and 242 kidnapped.
January	1959	— 184 civilians killed, 217 wounded and 197 kidnapped.
December	1959	— 143 civilians killed, 142 wounded and 78 kidnapped.

released about 7,000 from internment camps. It was thought that the total numbers interned were then in the region of 15,000. Hadj Messali was released at the same time, but forbidden to return to Algeria. Ben Bella and the other kidnapped FLN leaders were to be moved to a more comfortable prison.[1] These liberal gestures seemed to be offset by the heavy casualties inflicted by the French forces on the ALN in the field, but they were probably made with a special purpose in mind, as about this time secret contacts were being made between the French Government and the FLN.

Allegations that French forces used torture to extract information from captured Muslims erupted spasmodically. The Safeguard Commission investigated reports and complaints, but was not permitted to disclose its findings. However, a summary report on torture by the French Army by a Red Cross investigation committee, was 'leaked' to a newspaper[2] which published extracts on 4th January 1960, in which it said that torture *was* sometimes used by the French Army. In reply the French Government pointed out that seven Red Cross investigation committees in Algeria had been given full official co-operation, but that so far the FLN had refused to give the Red Cross any similar facilities.

The French continued to enforce such measures as they could, both actively and politically, to prevent arms and supplies reaching the ALN. For example, on 23rd December (1958) the authorities at Oran seized 40 tons of TNT from a foreign ship in port, alleging that it was destined for the ALN. On 8th April 1959 the French Navy intercepted a Czech freighter in the Mediterranean bound for Morocco, and took it to Oran where arms on board, amounting to 2,000 machine-guns, 12,000 rifles and stocks of ammunition, were confiscated. Strong protests from Czechoslovakia were ignored by the French, whose Navy continued to stop and search ships of any nation suspected of running munitions to the ALN as far afield as the Atlantic

[1] They were not actually moved from the Santé Prison, in Paris, to the island of Aix, near La Rochelle, until the first week in March 1959.
[2] *Le Monde*, Paris.

THE CHALLE PLAN

Ocean and the English Channel. Diplomatic protests at this activity were made by Britain, Western Germany, Yugoslavia, Bulgaria, Rumania, Poland and other countries.

In June (1959), the French scored a significant triumph in this sphere when she drew up a Black List of all countries supplying arms to the FLN, with details of transactions undertaken in this respect, and threatened to publish it unless the trade ceased. Italian and Western German firms, for example, had been supplying munitions, and Swiss banks had been transferring funds. This had a dramatic effect, and arms deliveries and transactions between the FLN and Western European and Communist countries suddenly dried up, the insurgent supply being reduced to only a small trickle from Arab countries, and what could be bought or obtained illegally and smuggled through. This gave rise to terror and intimidation of arms dealers and smugglers by both FLN and MNA agents in European countries to try to persuade them to collect and send munitions to Algeria.

Also operating for some time, in opposition to these insurgent agents, was a French extremist underground terrorist group, known as the Red Hand, which worked to prevent arms being sent to the ALN in Algeria by carrying out assassinations of arms dealers, smugglers, FLN and MNA agents and others concerned with this illicit trade. It was also allegedly responsible for damaging and sometimes sinking by explosions ships carrying, or about to carry, arms to the ALN.

The French claimed that by the end of 1959, of the some 15,000 active personnel of the ALN inside Algeria, only about one-third had modern arms.[1] This may not have been strictly accurate, but the supply of arms, which had formerly been ample for the numbers fighting in the field and undergoing training, almost dried up. From this time onwards a proportion

[1] French official sources had estimated that in January 1959, the ALN regular element inside Algeria numbered about 19,000. The figure may have been largely correct, but it most probably contained all the elements of the ALN, as the difference between the Moujahidines, the Moussebilines and the Fidayines had largely disappeared as the three elements by force of circumstances had merged either into the ALN or the ORU.

139

of the ALN fighters in Algeria were literally unarmed, while another proportion had only shot-guns, grenades and explosives. The French had most successfully hit at the insurgent arms supplies.

A flare-up of ALN activity in Algeria and some terrorism began in late January (1959) to influence Muslims and to show the persuasive power potential to the population before the March municipal elections. This included blowing up an oil train near Constantine, the first such successful attack of this nature for a year.

In the same month, Michel Debré, the Prime Minister, said that General de Gaulle's offer of a safe-conduct for representatives of the FLN to come to Paris to negotiate was still open, but it was not until April that de Gaulle made a belated answer to the FLN response, saying that talks must take place in Paris. By refusing to use the word 'integration', he implicitly rebuked the Ultras for their views. The following day, Ferhat Abbas replied, saying that the FLN was prepared to open negotiations in a neutral country without laying down any conditions. De Gaulle was temporarily silent. France warned the Soviet Union, India and certain other countries that she would break off diplomatic relations with them should they recognize the Provisional Algerian Government. This retarded general recognition, but tended to drive the Provisional Algerian Government into the orbit of Red China.

On 16th September, General de Gaulle made a broadcast offering the people of Algeria three choices: secession, complete integration or self-government in close association with France, within four years of the restoration of peace. He also renewed his offer of the Peace of the Brave, made originally in October 1958, which really only amounted to unconditional surrender.

America supported de Gaulle's suggestion, partly because she saw this as a means of ending the war in a non-colonial solution, and partly because, being deeply involved in the Cold War with the Soviet Union, she was anxious that France re-orientate her military effort to face the Soviet Union and that French military strength in Europe be built up for this purpose. President

Bourguiba of Tunisia at a press conference also approved de Gaulle's offer, as did Messali Hadj, who was directing his MNA from a Paris suburb.[1] It was estimated that there were 328,000 Algerian Muslims in France, of whom about 140,000 were in Paris alone, and that the MNA had the major influence over them.

On 28th September, the Provisional Algerian Government, in answer as it were to de Gaulle's offer, stated that it was prepared to open negotiations with the French for a cease-fire and for self-determination, but insisted that these conditions must include the complete withdrawal of French troops from Algeria. General de Gaulle made no public reply. It was obvious that the FLN did not want to see the future of Algeria handed over to the Muslim electorate at this stage, but was determined to win independence itself on behalf of the Algerian people.

At the same time, the Provisional Algerian Government mentioned wildly exaggerated Algerian Muslim civilian casualty figures. In answer, on 30th September, Delouvrier, the Delegate-General, issued figures to refute the FLN propaganda allegations. He said that the total security strength in Algeria, including police and auxiliaries, amounted to about 550,000. He also placed the total numbers of interned Muslims and refugees at about 110,000, and the total number of Muslim war victims at 150,000. Other figures of interest were released later at a press conference by General de Gaulle on 10th November. He said that of the 1·4 million men who had served with the French forces in Algeria, fewer than 13,000, less than one per cent, had been killed in battle, and this included Muslims. Up to 1st November, the fifth anniversary of the outbreak of the war, the insurgents had lost some 120,000 men killed, and about 60,000 had been captured.

The change of political emphasis vis-à-vis the Algerian problem as expounded by General de Gaulle was not made clear to the Army, which was still to some degree preaching integration of Europeans and Muslims into a French Algeria. By allowing

[1] That month FLN agents had made an unsuccessful attempt to assassinate Messali Hadj.

this political uncertainty to linger on, de Gaulle had hoped that perhaps a 'third force' of capable moderate Muslim politicians might emerge, with whom he could come to terms. The fact that General de Gaulle was prepared even to think about allowing Algeria to secede completely alarmed many, both in Algeria and France. In October, Marshal Juin, France's only living marshal, criticized de Gaulle's Algerian policy in an article in a magazine, but he was sharply informed that General de Gaulle wished all officers to avoid controversial political discussions.

Lack of success during 1959 prompted a re-shuffle of the Cabinet of the Provisional Algerian Government, which occurred on 19th January 1960, when 'extremists', such as Lamine-Debaghine (who was a pro-Nasser man) and Ben Khedda (who was regarded as being under the spell of Red China) were dropped. The newly shaped Cabinet, still under the leadership of Ferhat Abbas, considered to be composed of 'moderates', was perhaps more adaptable to a policy of negotiation.

Belkacem Krim, the Minister of the Armed Forces, was moved to Foreign Affairs, although he became a member of the new three-man 'Comité interministériel de guerre' (Inter-Ministerial War Committee), designed to direct all military activities. This Committee consisted of Belkacem Krim, Ben Tobbal and Abdel Hafid Boussouf, all former Wilaya commanders. Mohammed Said, who had been Chief of Staff of the ALN in eastern Algeria, was made a minister. As Aimirouche Ait Hamouda, who had been Chief of Staff to the ALN in western Algeria, had been killed, a single general staff for the whole of the country was formed under Houari Boumedienne. When Abdel Hafid Boussouf had been commanding Wilaya V, Houari Boumedienne had been his deputy, taking over the Wilaya when Abdel Hafid Boussouf was given a special responsibility in the CCE for communications. He also controlled the information network and the intelligence branch. Boussouf built up a counter-spy organization, aimed at detecting French agents in the insurgent organization.

1959 was a year in which the French Army and the Europeans, especially the Ultras, began to drift apart. It was a year in which secret contacts took place under cover of overt reluctance to negotiate by both sides. The Challe Plan had proved a military success and caused the FLN to think again about continuing to build up a large regular army with the object of one day fighting a final conventional battle, a Dien Bien Phu. Instead it was forced to wage guerilla warfare and to use terrorist tactics. There were signs that the Provisional Algerian Government was prepared to concentrate upon political means and pressure to gain a victory in its determination to wrest independence from France. Even so Boumedienne was given the task of forming a national army in Morocco and Tunisia. He set to work with a will, and soon became unpopular with the Wilaya commanders who alleged that he was deliberately depriving them of arms, supplies, and trained men.

CHAPTER 8

The European Insurrection

January 1960

Growing dissatisfaction amongst the Europeans over President de Gaulle's Algerian policy caused the Ultra organizations to become vocal and bitterly discontented.

At a press conference on 10th November 1959, President de Gaulle reaffirmed his promise (made on 16th September) that the Algerian people would be free to decide their own future once the process of pacification had been completed. This alarmed the Europeans, who would then clearly become an easily out-voted minority. The following day the Ultras formed the 'Comité d'Entente des Mouvements Nationaux' (Agreement Committee of National Movements), the CEMN, usually known as the Comité d'Entente, which consisted of five Ultra groups. Once formed, its representatives began negotiations with other European organizations, not so extreme in opinion, and the European ex-Servicemen's Associations. On the 20th, it was announced that these talks had been successful and that most of the European organizations had either joined, or become affiliated to, the new Comité d'Entente. So far the several Ultra and European groups had been divided in aims and outlook, and possessed differing degrees of determination and efficiency.

At the same press conference, President de Gaulle appealed to the FLN to order a cease-fire, and offered to allow any of its representatives to visit France, either openly or in secret, to negotiate, when they would be given a safe-conduct and travelling facilities. On the 20th, in reply, the FLN stated that it would not consider a cease-fire, but authorized a Five-Man body,[1] consisting of the FLN leaders in French detention, to open talks with the French Government. This was haughtily rejected by President de Gaulle, who made it clear that he would deal only with the military leaders of the insurrection and not those who were 'hors de combat', after which the FLN concentrated its diplomatic efforts towards the UN General Assembly debate on Algeria, which ended on 12th December.

A resurgence of terrorism in and around Algiers in which there were European victims upset the European population. The Government was blamed and the Army called upon to give more protection. There were 22 European deaths between 1st December and 10th January, and this gave impetus to the Comité d'Entente, which sponsored a general movement among the Europeans to group themselves together for defence against the ALN and Muslim terrorist attacks. In mid-December Georges Bidault, a prominent politician and former Minister, returned to Algeria to speak, when he denounced President de Gaulle's Algerian policy. Passions were warming up and were soon bubbling hotly just below the surface as Bidault's inflammatory words exacerbated the situation.

The loud protests at the lack of adequate army protection for the Europeans resulted in de Gaulle, on 14th January (1960), calling a conference, to be held in Paris on the 22nd and attended by Delouvrier, the Delegate-General, General Challe, the Commander-in-Chief, and the three regional commanders, General Massu, Olie and Gambiez.

Senior army officers in Algeria were also dissatisfied with de Gaulle's Algerian policy, and this more or less came to a head on 18th January, when a Western German newspaper[2] published an alleged interview by one of its correspondents with General Massu, in which Massu criticized President de Gaulle, saying that the French Army in Algeria did not understand

---

[1] This was to consist of Ben Bella, Hocine Ait Ahmed, Mohammed Boudiaf and Ben Khedda (all kidnapped in October 1956) and Rabah Bitat (arrested in January 1955).

[2] A Munich newspaper, *Suddeutsche Zeitung*.

him and that perhaps the Army had made a mistake in choosing him to be the leader of France. Massu was reported to have also said that the Army would never agree to leave Algeria. The same article contained a remark allegedly made by General Challe, confirming that the French Army would never abandon the country, and also going on to say that 'De Gaulle was the only man at our disposal in 1958'. General Massu was summoned to Paris the next day to explain. Both generals flatly denied ever saying such things, and it is probable that Massu had fallen into a trap certain Ultras had baited for him.

When General Massu, the Europeans' hero, departed for Paris the Comité d'Entente, and other European organizations, issued declarations supporting the General, and these, over the next few days, as Massu remained in Paris, developed into demonstrations. At first it was officially given out that General Massu, as formerly arranged, would attend President de Gaulle's conference (on the 24th), but suddenly on the afternoon of the 22nd it was announced that General Massu was relieved of his military and civil appointments, but that he would be given another post later on. General Crepin was to be his successor.

At first the news of General Massu's dismissal was held up by censorship, but it soon leaked through, coming as a bombshell to the Europeans, who were momentarily dumbfounded by this turn of events. The authorities in Algeria appealed for no strikes, but although most of the 23rd was fairly quiet, a number of shops were closed and there were mild demonstrations in the evening. It was, in fact, a day of plotting behind the scenes.

The next morning, the 24th, crowds of demonstrators appeared on the streets, many of whom wore their Territorial Unit uniforms. Several thousand Europeans belonged to the part-time Territorial Units, which formed a sort of urban reserve, and whose members took over certain static duties from the regular army for so many days a month. These units, although armed, clothed and equipped by the army, had become semi-autonomous and the military authorities did not really have full control over all of them. Ortiz, a European leader of the 'French National Front', addressed the crowds, and then had an interview with General Challe. Another prominent European leader, Lagaillarde, dressed in a paratroop Territorial Unit uniform, also inflamed the demonstrators, who by the afternoon were becoming rowdy, shouting anti-de Gaulle slogans and voicing their support for General Massu. A general strike was declared, and by evening barricades of large paving stones were being erected in certain parts of the city, under the urging and example of Lagaillarde. Manning the barricades in the streets, in the traditionally French revolutionary manner, appeals to Frenchmen and plays on their emotions, invoking unconscious ready-made sympathy and exuding glamour for the participants.

A gendarmerie unit charged a crowd of demonstrators, but was fired on by them, having to withdraw with casualties. Fourteen policemen and 6 civilians were killed in the exchange of shots, and 123 policemen and 20 civilians were wounded. The authorities put the blame for starting the firing on to Ortiz, who denied any part in the affray. By nightfall there had arisen two fairly large barricaded areas in Algiers, one, under Lagaillarde, around the university buildings, and the other under Ortiz, close by. Within these barricades were up to 1,500 Europeans, many of whom were armed and in their Territorial Unit uniforms.

General Challe ordered a curfew in Algiers, and in the evening, as the situation became worse, declared a 'state of siege'. Censorship was imposed, and messages from Algeria were limited to official ones. General Challe wanted to resign, but President de Gaulle refused to allow this, instead ordering him to restore order quickly; something that was easier said than done. De Gaulle took to the radio to inform the people of France about events in Algiers.

The Army, in the form of General Massu's 10th Paratroop Division, closed in around the two barricaded areas, but took no other action. The Europeans within the barricades were able to make contact with the crowds, and in fact came and went over the barricades as they pleased, the surrounding soldiers making no move to prevent this inter-communication or to stop open contact. In some cases, fresh insurgents went into, and stayed in, the barricaded areas, and in others a few left to return to their homes. While the paratroops made no aggressive move against the European insurgents, but merely held a watching brief, the Army as a whole also remained passive and mute, and did not show any sign of open sympathy or of coming out on the side of the Ultras, as most probably had been hoped or expected. Lagaillarde and Ortiz and other leaders called for a strict enforcement of the general strike. The Europeans still thought that violent demonstrations would help them attain their ends.

During the day, the numbers of European insurgents behind the barricades increased until they exceeded 2,000, and they became more organized and orderly under Lagaillarde and Ortiz. Other major cities in Algeria remained quiet, waiting to see what the outcome of the struggle in Algiers would be. During the evening, more army reinforcements, again mainly paratroops of the 10th Paratroop Division, moved into Algiers to strengthen the surrounding cordon, but open contact between the European insurgents and the crowds continued. The general strike was being rigidly enforced by the Ultras. The police, who had been repulsed with casualties in their initial attempts to dismantle the barricades, asked for military assistance to do this, which was not forthcoming, the majority of senior army officers being unwilling to order their soldiers to fire on Frenchmen.

In Paris, it was suspected that there were divided counsels in President de Gaulle's Cabinet on the use of force to quell this insurrection. It was thought that Malreaux, the Minister of Information, led the faction that advocated the use of force, while others, probably led by Soustelle, were against this course, urging negotiations instead. De Gaulle secretly sent his Prime Minister, Debré, to Algeria to find out what was really happening, and to sound out loyalties.

The same situation—watchful waiting between the barricaded European insurgents and the surrounding paratroops—

continued the next day, and indeed for several days. For the first two or three there was a distinct friendliness between the paratroops and the insurgents in the barricades, and many paratroops went inside them to drink with the Europeans. It was alleged that army ambulances were lent to the insurgents, who used them to tour the city to collect arms and ammunition, and to bring them into the barricaded areas.

The general strike soon began to inconvenience the people in the city as uncollected refuse accumulated and other public services did not function. On the 26th, both Delouvrier and General Challe broadcast appeals for a return to order, Challe promising that Algeria would remain French. Several thousand Europeans demonstrated their support for the insurgents in front of the barricades, many of them wearing their Territorial Unit uniforms. That night an Ultra commando group from Lagaillarde's barricade entered a military hospital and freed four men convicted of the attempt on General Salan's life (in January 1957 by firing a bazooka) who were being treated there.

Debré returned to France from Algeria convinced that the generals would not order their soldiers to fire on Frenchmen, and several had told him that this was a political, and not a military, problem. Both army officers and Europeans demanded a retraction of de Gaulle's offer of self-determination to the people of Algeria, and that more positive steps be taken to keep Algeria French. Several ministers submitted their resignations, but President de Gaulle refused to accept them, demanding that they stay on and do their duty. Rumours of dissension within the Cabinet continued, and it was believed that Soustelle was rallying support against the use of force to quell the European insurgents in Algiers.

On the 28th, Delouvrier announced that he and General Challe were moving their headquarters out of Algiers to Reghala, an air force camp about 16 miles from the city, so as to be able to maintain freedom of action. Delouvrier called upon Muslims to go out into the streets to demonstrate for President de Gaulle, but this was not heeded. Had it been, bloodshed would have been inevitable. The Muslims of Algeria watched this tragedy from the sidelines without interfering.

Within Algiers the same suspended, confused situation obtained. Troops surrounded the barricaded areas, but no one in authority had given them any orders to fire, or to take firmer action against the European insurgents. There were considerable doubts as to whether such orders would have been obeyed, and in any case senior officers hesitated to put this to the test. There were strikes and demonstrations in favour of the European insurgents and against de Gaulle in other cities in Algeria by this time, but only in Oran were barricades erected.

Owing to army censorship on news from Algeria, the majority of Frenchmen had not fully realized how serious this revolt was until the 27th. Up till then they were under the impression merely that the European insurgents had barricaded themselves in a small sector of Algiers. They did not comprehend that the rebels held a fairly prominent area, controlled the public services and the opening and closing of shops, and organized strikes and demonstrations, while the army was standing passively by, its officers uncertain as to whether their soldiers would obey orders.

On the 29th, after considering Debré's report on the situation in Algiers, President de Gaulle broadcast to the French nation, making an especial appeal to the army for loyalty, and demanding unconditional surrender of the European insurgents. He insisted that it was the Government's firm intention to restore order and not modify its Algerian policy. He said that the Algerian people should have a free choice of their destiny, and that self-determination was a worthy aim. Once the true facts were realized, expressions of support and sympathy began to come in to President de Gaulle in an ever-increasing volume. These coincided with many arrests of extreme right-wing suspects in Paris and other parts of France.

By this time, the soldiers of the 10th Paratroop Division, elements of which had been in Algiers so long that they were suspected of at least being in open sympathy with the Europeans, were replaced by other troops (of the 25th Division), brought in specially from the Constantine region. Now the army attitude towards the European insurgents and the demonstrators hardened, and free and open contact between them was gradually broken off. Any possible sympathy and support from the Army as a whole—in reality only watchful passiveness—was abruptly withdrawn from the insurgents, who were now besieged within their barricades, and the sympathetic European crowds were kept at a distance. The general strike also began to dissolve.

On the 30th, orders were issued by General Challe directing all personnel in the Territorial Units to report for duty. Later that day, angry European crowds assembled near the barricades, and several attempts were made to break through the cordon of soldiers. Only one was temporarily successful. Army pressure was intensified; and, deprived of the active support of the European crowds, the insurgents became short of food.

Seeing that all was hopeless, the leaders, Lagaillarde and Ortiz, agreed to talk to military representatives, and on 1st February about 780 of the European insurgents surrendered to units of the Foreign Legion that were surrounding the barricades. The remainder had escaped over the roof-tops or through the sewers. About 420 of them were taken into custody, including Lagaillarde. Many had left the barricades before the army cordon had become too restrictive. The same day the men of the Territorial Units were stood down and told to resume their civilian occupations.

The European insurrection of January 1960 against President de Gaulle's Algerian policy was over. By patience and adroit handling of events and people, de Gaulle had won without having to order French soldiers to fire on French citizens.[1] Spontaneous, emotional violence had been no match for de Gaulle's political acumen.

Lagaillarde, together with other prominent personalities of the European insurrection, were flown to Paris to await trial. Ortiz, the other leader, had disappeared, as had others. About

[1] Although 24 people had been killed and 250 injured in the European insurrection.

120 of the insurgents were mustered into the French Foreign Legion to be formed into the so-called 'Alcazar Commando', but they were tacitly allowed to return to their homes one by one, and on 4th March this unit was dissolved.

On 2nd February, President de Gaulle's Government was granted special powers for one year to maintain order in both France and Algeria. Three days later de Gaulle reorganized his Cabinet, dismissing Soustelle. On the 4th, Delouvrier had dissolved a number of Ultra organizations, including the French National Front, led by Ortiz, formed in June 1958, which had about 14,000 members.

The Territorial Units, amounting to about 130,000 men, of whom about 30,000 were in Algiers, were disbanded, and the commander arrested. Former members were still made liable for recall for service up to 20 days a year if required, but under different conditions. They would no longer, even if mobilized, constitute the semi-autonomous force they had previously been.

Another measure taken was to dissolve the 5th Bureau, the Army's psychological warfare branch, and most of its duties were transferred to the regional commanders. A new body, the Interservice Co-ordination Centre, was set up to take its place, and to ensure that psychological warfare did not get out of control. The French Army in Algeria had been engaged in psychological warfare since 1955, the 5th Bureau being formed in November 1957, to be reorganized two years later when it was placed under joint military and civil control. Throughout its existence its activities had been criticized, as had been its methods, but it had achieved considerable results in dealing with Algerian insurgents, persuading many to reverse their views through 'brain washing'. It was bitterly hated, and greatly feared, by the FLN, which used every propaganda weapon possible against it. President de Gaulle's main objection to the 5th Bureau seemed to be that its officers developed political convictions and theories similar to those held by the Europeans, and so often contrary to his own.

The police in Algeria were reorganized and brought under the direct control of the Delegate-General. Also, certain changes were made in the administration of justice, the penal code was amended and wider powers were given to the Prefects. Colonel Godard, the Director-General of the Security Services in Algeria since May 1958, a former 5th Bureau chief, was replaced by a policeman.

A new Committee of Algerian Affairs was established under the chairmanship of President de Gaulle, and a policy was pursued of gradually giving over a larger share of the administration of the country to Muslims. The Army continued to control certain regions where the ALN was most active, but other sectors were handed back to civilian authorities to look after.

Senior army officers did not altogether escape President de Gaulle's displeasure, and on 10th February, for example, three generals were relieved of their commands for their passive parts in the European insurrection. Other senior officers were selectively weeded out, but for the time being General Challe, the Commander-in-Chief in Algeria, retained his position. He was eventually retired in April 1960.

CHAPTER 9

War Weariness

January 1960—April 1961

Once President de Gaulle had conceded the principle of self-determination to the people of Algeria, the FLN and the ALN more or less stopped fighting the French Army seriously, and instead began to rely mainly upon political and diplomatic methods and pressures to gain their objective. De Gaulle had outpointed the Provisional Algerian Government, as his offer could only be interpreted as meaning that one day the Muslim Algerian majority would be able to elect a government of its own choice, a logical step towards complete independence. This gained him moral support from America, Britain and other Western nations, and also the cautious approval of both Tunisia and Morocco. The threatening to publish a Black List of countries supplying arms had been a bad blow to the FLN, and now this had followed. Rather taken back, the FLN was only able to make weak counter-proposals. Support from abroad for France was rallying, and that for the FLN was weakening. Moreover, France became a nuclear power, exploding her first nuclear device on 13th February 1960 at Reggan in the Sahara.

This did not mean to say that insurgent fighting inside Algeria ceased. On the contrary, the flurry of small guerilla actions, behind which the Provisional Algerian Government worked unceasingly, and later a revival of terrorism, were maintained as a camouflage shield. The idea of building up and training a large regular force with the ultimate purpose of one day meeting and defeating the French Army in battle, as the Viet Minh had done at Dien Bien Phu, was modified. There were so many obstacles. Apart from the shortages of arms, equipment and ammunition, and recruits (despite protests to the contrary), there was little practical prospect of large conventional forces breaking through the Morice Line to get at the French Army, so this change of plan was very much a course dictated by necessity.

The year 1960 was one in which both President de Gaulle and the Provisional Algerian Government made moves and counter-moves. De Gaulle was still striving, through his devious system of elections, to reach the Muslim people in Algeria over the heads of the FLN, but at the same time he made secret contacts with this organization.

On 30th January, the African Peoples' Congress, meeting in Tunis, called upon the governments of the independent African states to create a corps of African volunteers to fight with the ALN. This suggestion simmered for a while, as the FLN gauged de Gaulle's reaction, and it was not until 11th April that the Provisional Algerian Government announced its decision to accept foreign volunteers 'of whatever origin' to fight the French in Algeria. It added that for the time being priority would be given to technicians. Publicity was given to this move mainly by the Provisional Algerian Government and Muslim states. Recruiting offices were opened in Cairo and other Arab capitals, and boastful announcements were made of the numbers of volunteers forthcoming. The fact was that this grandiose scheme did not come to fruition and gradually fizzled out, but it caused hidden anxiety on the part of the French at the thought of the war in Algeria being internationalized in this way.

Belkacem Krim, Foreign Minister in the Provisional Algerian Government, went to Red China to press unsuccessfully the cause of foreign volunteers to fight in Algeria. However, it is believed that he obtained promises of more money and some material aid, which went some way to offset the disappointment of the cessation of supplies, arms and aid from Iron Curtain countries. The Soviet Union, for example, had not yet recognized the Provisional Algerian Government.

From the insurgent point of view the war in Algeria needed

a new lease of life and required some sort of stimulant to be injected into the ALN to revive morale and to try and redress the unfavourable military situation. The bulk of the armed and organized regular element of the ALN, amounting to about 10,000 trained men in 10 battalions, with some light artillery, was locked up in Tunisia because of rigid French control of the frontier, and could not be committed into action.

Local elections were held in Algeria between the 27th and 29th of May, when about 56 per cent of the electorate voted, mainly supporting President de Gaulle. This was a further stage in his manœuvres to reach past the FLN to get at the people, as had really been his policy from the beginning. The FLN by terror and threats tried to persuade the Algerian Muslims to abstain from voting, but were only partially successful, although three candidates had been killed before the election itself. In the Casbah in Algiers, for example, only 30 per cent voted, while in Setif, the home town of Ferhat Abbas, only 14 per cent turned out. In the areas where the poll was heavier, French army trucks and personnel had gone out into the countryside, almost forcibly bringing in the people to vote.

Secret contacts between the French and the Provisional Algerian Government bore fruit to the extent that the representatives of both met for preliminary talks at Melun, near Paris, between the 25th and 29th of June. The object was to pave the way, and make arrangements for, a visit to France of a full FLN delegation to discuss a cease-fire and other political questions. These talks ended without any agreement being reached. They had been further complicated by Messali Hadj, the leader of the MNA, who wanted to take part in all negotiations for a cease-fire, claiming that he had a right to do so as he still had a fighting contingent in Algeria. In fact this amounted merely to a few hundred scattered fighters, the remnants of the MNA National Army of the Algerian People. The FLN had taken exception to Messali Hadj's demands.

On 4th July, the Provisional Algerian Government rejected the French terms for a visit of a FLN delegation to France, denouncing them as far too restrictive. Apparently, the FLN had expected that members of its delegation would be free to travel about France, and also to interview and consult all sorts of sympathizers, including Ben Bella and the other detained FLN leaders. It was also said that the FLN was not too keen on a cease-fire in Algeria yet, as it had not obtained full support from all the Muslims, and feared the results of any free elections. This may have had some substance.

After the failure of the Melun negotiations, there was increased agitation in France to make efforts to renew contacts with the FLN again with the object of at least obtaining a cease-fire, if not a complete ending to the war in Algeria. French moderate and 'middle of the road' political parties now began to add their voices to those of the left wing in these demands. A dull war weariness began to seep over all France. For long there had been dissatisfaction over the conduct of the Algerian war, that had been dragging on for six years, and now that French conscripts were used in Algeria[1] its implications reached into practically every French home. Already, on 1st February, a one-hour token strike in Paris had been staged by trade unions and student bodies. Then the teachers' unions called for negotions with the FLN without any pre-conditions at all.

In September, a declaration, which became known as the 'Manifesto of the 121', was issued concerning the right of conscripts to refuse to serve in Algeria. It was signed by 121 teachers, civil servants, writers and artists, all intellectuals, and others with left-wing views, but not by any Communists. This caused a storm of controversy, and eventually action was taken against the signatories. A few were charged with incitement to mutiny and desertion, the teachers and civil servants were dismissed from their posts, and the artists and writers were banned from working for the State television and broadcasting services.

The Manifesto of 121 prompted a counter-manifesto, which was issued on 6th October, originally signed by 185 people with right-wing opinions, including Marshal Juin. Eventually it

[1] The Indo-China war, 1945-54, had been more remote from the people of France as conscripts were not sent to this theatre, the fighting being carried out by regular or volunteer forces.

gathered 300 signatures. On 17th October, the Assembly of French Cardinals and Bishops issued a statement on the Algerian War condemning desertion and subversive activities, but casting doubts on certain practices. It disapproved of torture and emphasized that orders of this nature should be disobeyed.

During September and October, when the controversy of the Manifesto of the 121 was raging, stricter measures were taken by the Government, and many left-wing periodicals containing adverse articles on the Algerian War, such as those mentioning or alleging torture by French soldiers, were confiscated by the police.

The fact that 1960 was a year of political trials connected with Algerian events brought, and kept, many unpalatable and often disturbing and unsuspected facts before the public eye. The issue was kept at white-hot temperature by the opening of the 'Barricades Trial' of the leaders of the European insurrection of January 1960, which began early in November, and dragged on until March (1961). Lagaillarde, released on 'provisional liberty', absconded, with three other Europeans also on trial for similar offences, to Spain. Ortiz, the other prominent Ultra leader, was known to be in the Balearic Islands.

Voicing adverse criticism on the Algerian issue was one thing, but disturbing revelations in 1960 made it evident that a few French extremists were prepared to go much further; on 24th February, it was announced that the DST, the security police, had arrested 10 members of a 'support network' that had been assisting the FLN by sheltering Algerian Muslims wanted by the police, carrying messages and transferring funds for the FLN. More arrests followed in the ensuing days. This became known as the Jeanson Case, after the alleged leader of this subversive organization, who, with others, had evaded arrest. This was the first real intimation to the people of France that a few of their countrymen were actively helping the 'rebels'. During the year, three more similar subversive French organizations, whose objects were to assist French deserters and help the FLN, were unearthed by the police.

Further details came to light on 15th April, when Jeanson

158

gave a secret press conference 'somewhere in Paris', at which he alleged that his organization, despite arrests, was largely intact and still operating. He said that during the previous three years it had arranged for the transfer abroad of funds for the FLN, amounting to about £300,000 a month, and that it had assisted or harboured over 3,000 French deserters. The trial of the arrested members of the Jeanson Organization opened on 5th September, and ended with some being sentenced to terms of imprisonment and fines, and others being acquitted. On 8th October, the Swiss police admitted that they had just expelled Jeanson from Switzerland, but would not disclose to where he had been deported.

Another distinguished military critic of President de Gaulle's Algerian policy, apart from Marshal Juin, was General Salan, recently retired, who had taken up residence in Algiers. On 14th September, he issued a statement attacking de Gaulle's policy, insisting that Algeria was part of France, and that no one had any right to give away French territory. Summoned to Paris, General Salan was told that he was forbidden to return to Algeria, so at the end of October he slipped quietly away to Spain. This broke the last senior-officer link with the Europeans who had taken part in the events of 13th May 1958. The other army officers who had played prominent parts, such as General Massu, had all been posted away from Algeria.

As a reaction to the French attitude to the Melun negotiations, and in an attempt to gain material and moral assistance, Ferhat Abbas led a Provisional Algerian Government delegation to both Moscow and Peking in late September and early October. He was successful in persuading the Soviet Union to recognize his Government (on 7th October), but obtained little else. The Soviet Union was becoming a trifle embarrassed by the Algerian War. Khrushchev urged negotiation to end the struggle and was in favour of the FLN resuming the Melun negotiations. The Soviet Union did however promise to send some non-military supplies, such as food, clothing and tractors, and also to supply the ALN with arms, once it was in control of a piece of Algerian territory. Other Iron Curtain countries, following the Soviet lead, were similarly unhelpful, although it was agreed to continue to give medical facilities to seriously wounded ALN fighters, of whom there were already 'several hundreds' currently being treated in Iron Curtain country hospitals.

In Red China, Ferhat Abbas was slightly more successful, being given VIP treatment in Peking, where he was received by the President, Liu Shao-chi, Mao Tse-tung and Chou En-lai, although he did not obtain arms and aircraft asked for. Chou En-lai issued a communiqué saying that Red China was 'ready to lend total assistance and support to the just struggle of the Algerian people'. Mao Tse-tung is supposed to have advised Ferhat Abbas[1] against the use of torture, and instead to rely upon an 'unceasing effort of persuasion'. Mao Tse-tung also advised him to insist upon real and solid independence, and not to accept any compromise.

As before, cash was given, which had formerly enabled the FLN to purchase munitions on the markets of Europe, and this time some arms were promised; but the following month, the Provisional Algerian Government could neither persuade Tunisia nor Morocco to ship them through their ports. It was estimated that by the end of the year (1960), by the time the additional Red Chinese assistance became effective, the FLN budget was running at roughly $80 million annually, of which half was provided by Red China. The other half was contributed by Muslim countries. An additional silent figure, perhaps as much as another $30 million, was extracted by terror and blackmail from Algerian Muslim workers in France and from other subversive sources. Also, further sums were prised from Muslims in Algeria, again by terror and blackmail.

Continuing his efforts to reach past the Provisional Algerian Government, which he insisted had no mandate from the Algerian people but had imposed itself on them, President de Gaulle held a press conference on 5th September, at which he

---

[1] According to a report of an interview with Ferhat Abbas, published in a Tunisian weekly journal, *Afrique-Action*.

made further vague utterances on his policy for an 'Algerian-Algeria'. He repeated his former offers to negotiate with the FLN, this time without the 'four-year period' after a cease-fire for a referendum, and he blamed the FLN leaders for the failure of the Melun negotiations.

This was followed, on 4th November, by a broadcast to the nation, when he spoke of an Algerian-Algeria, not governed by France, that could secede, and made it obvious that he was determined to carry through his ideas and at a faster pace. This broadcast provoked strong criticism by right-wing elements, both in Algeria and France. Delouvrier asked to be relieved of his post, and on the 23rd was replaced by Jean Morin. In November, John Kennedy became the President of America; in 1957, he had said that the 'independence of Algeria was the first essential step in North Africa'. This gave hope and inspiration to the Provisional Algerian Government.

President de Gaulle sent Pierre Mesmer, Minister of the Armed Forces, and General Ely, the Armed Forces Chief of Staff, to Algeria to survey the prospects of a unilateral cease-fire, and to inform the Army that the ultimate solution must be an independent republic.

On 8th December, President de Gaulle began a visit to Algeria to sound out and encourage both the Army and the Algerian Muslims in preparation for the national referendum, due to take place in that country the following month (January 1961). More army officers suspected of being actively against his policy were removed from Algeria, and some from the Army altogether. Now thoroughly suspect and unpopular with the Europeans, and especially the Ultras, huge demonstrations were organized against him, particularly in Algiers and Oran, in which two cities there were also strikes. (De Gaulle did not visit Algiers on this occasion.) The 10th was a bad day of demonstrations and disorders, the day Algerian Muslims, under threats and pressure from the FLN, came out on the streets in counter-demonstrations against both the Ultras and President de Gaulle. The red, white and Green FLN flag, with a red crescent and star imposed on it, was seen everywhere, and Muslims sacked European shops and premises, and burnt cars on the streets. Disorder had given place to violence and destruction.

The Europeans were stunned and astonished at the Muslim action, so well organized by the FLN. This was the first outbreak of Muslim violence in Algiers since the Casbah had been cleared by General Massu in 1957. Unprepared and unsuspecting, the Europeans were at a loss and leaderless at this critical juncture. General Salan and Lagaillarde were in Spain, and Ortiz in the Balearic Islands, and French diplomatic pressure was exerted to persuade the Spanish authorities to prevent their leaving. Soustelle was away visiting America.

Seeing the passions and violence his presence engendered, greeted with shouts of 'Algérie Française' from Europeans wherever he went, President de Gaulle cut short his visit, returning to France on the 12th.

The Army was used against Ultra mobs in Algiers and Oran when they attempted to form barricades, and for the first time in the history of Algeria, French soldiers opened fire on French citizens, killing 3 and wounding 15. Quiet was not restored until the 13th, by which time 90 Muslims and 6 Europeans had been killed in Algiers and 18 Muslims killed in Oran, 317 Muslims and 53 Europeans injured in Algiers, and 100 more (Europeans and Muslims) injured in Oran. President de Gaulle blamed the Europeans for the disorders and punished all he could. For instance, civil servants who had taken part in the strike were dismissed, and the Ultra organization, 'The Algerian Front', was dissolved.

Broadcasting from Tunis on the 16th, a jubilant Ferhat Abbas instructed the Algerian Muslims to call off their demonstrations, saying they had been a success and had achieved their object. The FLN had now consolidated its hold over the Muslim population, and no longer feared independent elections. Proof of this had just been given.

President de Gaulle had hoped to impress on the Army in Algeria that it had two main tasks, one of which was security, meaning prosecuting the Algerian war, and the other was fraternization to gain the co-operation of the Muslims. He had hoped to win the support of the majority of the Muslims and separate them from the FLN, so that they might eventually produce a moderate leadership or tier of politicians that could negotiate a new relationship with France. The sight of so many FLN flags and slogans made him realize that this was no longer possible.

The inability of the French Army, despite an intensive civic programme that had been in progress since 1958 supported by the 5th Bureau, until it had been disbanded in January 1960, to win over the Muslim masses to the idea of a French-Algeria, convinced de Gaulle that this policy had not only failed, but was no longer realistic. He suspended the political side of the civic programme, mainly because he was anxious lest the Army in Algeria as a whole become politically-minded and too immersed in politics.

General Crepin, General Challe's successor as Commander-in-Chief in Algeria, continued to use similar strategy and tactics, adhering to the principles of the Challe Plan, but only two large-scale operations were launched during 1960, one in July and the other in October. It was not the policy to mount big sweeps against the ALN whilst negotiations or contacts, both open and secret, were in progress. On 23rd July, the first operation was begun in the Ouarsenis, where the ALN had managed to re-establish its military and political organizations again after the French offensive of 1959. When it came to an end it was announced that during its course 669 insurgents had been killed, 464 captured, 282 members of the ORU arrested, several tons of munitions seized and 20,000 people moved into regroupment centres.[1]

The second operation, beginning on 13th October, took place in the Aures Mountains, where it was estimated that the ALN had between 1,800 and 2,000 armed fighters. On the 24th, an ALN unit taken by surprise lost 160 killed in a few hours' fighting. On the 28th, when the operation terminated,

---

[1] By July 1960, there were about 1½ million Algerian Muslims in regroupment centres, about 11,000 in internment camps, and another ½ million were huddled into 'bidonvilles' (shanty towns) near the cities.

it was announced that about 400 insurgents had been killed and another 100 captured.

In the course of the year there were incidents on both the Tunisian and Moroccan frontiers. The French alleged they were fired on from Tunisian territory on occasions, and the Tunisians alleged that the French Army laid booby-traps on Tunisian soil that killed Tunisians. The Moroccan frontier tended to be a little quieter, but there were infringements. The most notable one, that received some publicity, occurred on 28th September, when the French Army shelled a Moroccan village just to the north of Oudjda, as a group of ALN fighters were attempting to sabotage the electrified and mined frontier barrier.

In February 1961, General Gambiez assumed the position of Commander-in-Chief of the forces in Algeria. There were still nearly 500,000 French troops in the country, as well as about 160,000 Algerian Muslims in or with the French Army. Of the Muslims, only about 50,000 were in fighting units, while the remainder were in home-guard type formations, often near regroupment centres, under French officers. No large-scale operations were mounted in the early part of 1961 owing to both secret and open negotiations being arranged between the French Government and the FLN. There was, however, widespread guerilla activity, the number of incidents of all sorts still averaging over 3,000 a year.[1]

Some activity centred along the Moroccan frontier as several ALN units tried to break through the electrified barrier to get into Algeria, mainly in the region between Tlemcen and Ain Sefra. On 21st February, one ALN unit was caught and wiped out, losing 145 killed and captured. On 30th March, it was officially said that none of the ALN units breaking through into Algeria since February had been able to penetrate more than 12 miles from the Moroccan border without being detected, and that most had been wiped out or dispersed within hours. To the east, one of the biggest actions occurred on 15th February, when 141 insurgents were killed in a week-long operation near Batna.

[1] In 1957, for example, there had been about 8,000 incidents.

Although generally the ALN operated in small groups of 6 to 12 men the better to avoid French searching troops and to carry out guerilla tactics, there was a move in parts of the country where there was determined leadership to return to the katiba, the company-sized unit. The new pattern was smaller, consisting of between 30 and 40 men, and was a self-contained unit able to march at least 25 miles across country to out-distance the 'commandos de chasse'. These new-type katibas also infiltrated back into the so-called pacified zones whenever they could.

Shortage of arms and ammunition was now a serious problem in the ALN, which was believed to have only about 15,000 modern infantry weapons, such as machine-guns and rifles, of which up to two-thirds were with the waiting ALN battalions in Tunisia and Morocco. This restricted ALN activity inside Algeria. The heavy casualties inflicted by the French Army whenever it encountered ALN units, still running at the ap-proximate rate of 30,000 a year, caused an inevitable lowering of morale. Many ALN units that had fought well paused and lived on their former reputations, doing as little fighting as possible, concentrating upon conserving themselves and their arms. Recruits, who often had to be taken straight from the village militia (the Fidayines), since sufficient trained replace-ments for casualties were unable to get back into Algeria from either Tunisia or Morocco, were frequently reluctant and of poor material. In short, from an ALN point of view, the war in Algeria was running down and a defensive mentality began to seep through its ranks. Few aggressive actions of any magni-tude were mounted.

The French boasted that they had more Algerian Muslims (about 50,000 excluding home guards) fighting for them than had the ALN altogether. It was estimated that in the early part of 1961 the ALN had about 16,000 men in camps in Tunisia, about 8,000 in Morocco, and about 15,000, of whom only about 7,600 were armed, in Algeria. There were also in Algeria about 10,000 supporters, mainly ORU personnel, terrorists and others in the village militia, the Fidayines. FLN radio constantly called upon the Algerian Muslims with the French Army to desert, but the desertion rate seldom exceeded about 300 a month.

During the summer of 1960 there had been a revival of terrorist incidents, following the conviction and execution of Algerian nationalists during July and August, but generally terrorism declined during the year, it being officially stated that there were only 729 incidents in the month of November, as compared with 954 in the November of 1959.

Perhaps the worst incident of this nature occurred when ALN terrorists fired on people bathing on a beach at Chenoua, some 50 miles to the west of Algiers, killing 14. This was a prestige raid, partly caused by disappointment of the failure of the Melun negotiations, and partly to counter French propaganda that the FLN and the ALN were finished as an effective force. The last instance of a serious bomb explosion by ALN terrorists in Algiers occurred on 15th February (1961) when one man was killed and 20 more injured. After this, the Ultras began to be active in this sphere. Using plastic explosive they had begun to instigate explosions after the failure of the European insurrection in January 1960, spasmodically at first, and then in a more regular crescendo, until by April (1961) plastic bombs placed by Ultra terrorists were exploding in Algiers at the rate of three a day. The Ultras using these plastic bombs became known as 'plastiqueurs'.

Plastic explosive had been developed in World War II, and was a putty-like substance made by mixing two explosives[1] into a compound that could be exploded either electrically or by a fuse. The plastic explosive material was malleable, in that it could be moulded or cut into small pieces, which enabled it to be carried easily and secretly. It was also slightly adhesive and would stick conveniently on to, or under, a ledge, wall, lamppost or letter-box.

The referendum for self-determination[2] of the Algerian

[1] Hexogen and TNT.

[2] The referendum read: 'Do you approve the Bill submitted to the French people by the President of the Republic concerning the self-determination of the Algerian population and the organization of the public powers in Algeria prior to self-determination?'

people was held in France on 8th January 1961, and in Algeria between the 6th and the 8th. The FLN did not like the idea at all as it looked like sweeping its political platform from under its feet, and on 1st January Ferhat Abbas, broadcasting from Tunis, appealed to the Algerian Muslims not to vote, but to stay away from the polling booths. He was partially successful, as in the cities and towns most Muslims abstained, but in the countryside they were rounded up and taken in army trucks to vote. Just over half the electorate (58 per cent) voted, of whom the majority were in favour of de Gaulle's proposal. Almost all the Europeans voted against it. The total result was an overwhelming 'yes' for President de Gaulle, but it was said that there were two referendums, one in France for de Gaulle, and one in Algeria for the FLN.

Fortified by his referendum triumph, President de Gaulle was able to ignore right-wing elements in France and the Ultras in Algeria. A partition plan put forward by some Ultras, for instance, as a makeshift, suggesting that coastal cities and areas should remain French, could be shrugged off owing to the massive abstentions of the Muslim city dwellers. De Gaulle realized that the FLN had suddenly become a power to be seriously reckoned with in Algeria, and he went ahead with his secret contacts with the Provisional Algerian Government. In mid-January, Ferhat Abbas claimed that the massive Muslim boycott of the referendum in Algeria proved the authority of the FLN, and that he was ready to begin negotiations for a solution to the Algerian problem. President Bourguiba, of Tunisia,[1] was active in arranging go-betweens and contacts, and soon the secret negotiations became more open, being aimed at arranging a meeting on 7th April of French and FLN delegations at Evian-les-Bains, a town on the French side of Lake Geneva.

De Gaulle no longer demanded a cease-fire before political talks, and negotiations seemed to be progressing favourably until 27th March, when Messali Hadj, the leader of the MNA, said he was preparing a MNA delegation on the same lines as the anticipated FLN one. Joxe, the Minister in charge of

[1] President Bourguiba visited President de Gaulle in France in March 1961.

Algerian Affairs, who had been nominated to lead the French delegation, intimated that he would meet the MNA on an equal footing with the FLN. On the 31st, the Provisional Algerian Government backed out, refusing to share the negotiating table with MNA representatives, and claiming that the FLN had the sole right to speak for the people of Algeria. It was true that by this time Messali Hadj had lost most of his influence and contacts in Algeria. He also favoured some form of close association with France, which did not meet with FLN approval. Also, the FLN suspected that the French might insist on keeping the Sahara, with all its newly discovered wealth, and were a little wary.

At a press conference in mid-April, President de Gaulle said he had given the FLN a choice between freedom in association with France or partition. The partition plan was favoured by the Europeans, but the FLN came down heavily against it.

By April 1961 the situation in Algeria was tense and watchful. The Ultras and the Europeans watched the negotiation moves with suspicion and fear. President Kennedy's known views, great prestige and background influence caused further European depression. Such pro-French officials and 'tame' politicians as continued to function began to veer over to the FLN point of view one by one, speaking less and less of an 'Algérie Française'.

The French Army, weary of the war and unhappy in its role in Algeria, had been fairly passive as no large-scale operations were to be mounted lest they rupture negotiations, but spasmodic ambushes and incidents, spread wide across the country, continued to take a steady daily toll of dead and wounded.

Short of arms, supplies and recruits, the ALN units in Algeria were content to concentrate upon survival and political activities, and they were also comparatively passive. There were more armed ALN fighters outside Algeria than within its borders, but the heavily French-guarded frontiers made physical contact between the two hazardous in the extreme.

CHAPTER 10

The Generals' Revolt

April 1961

Early on the morning of 22nd April 1961, a voice suddenly announced over the Algiers radio that the armed forces had taken control of the Algerian-Saharan territory. Operation 'Green Light' was under way, and the third serious revolt in Algeria against the authority of the French Government was in progress, this time led by Salan, Challe, Jouhaud and Zeller, four retired generals.

Open gossip about an 'Algerian Republic' in the negotiation discussions for the approaching Evian Talks caused the plotters to act quickly if they wanted Algeria to remain French and not to be handed over to the FLN. It is believed that it was not until 11th April that Generals Challe and Zeller, who were in France at the time, and who were throughout the leading planners, put the wheels of revolt into motion. This time there was only a small number of plotters, perhaps a dozen or so, as this was considered to be the most sensible number both from the security and planning aspects, but it was confidently anticipated that once the revolt was launched hundreds of army officers would join in, and it would have massive European support. General Salan, who was in Spain, was more remote from the centre of the plotting, as was to some extent General Jouhaud, who was living in Algeria.

General Challe, a former Commander-in-Chief in Algeria and the originator of the successful Challe Plan, was probably the 'brains' of the plot. He had resigned in November 1959, in order to vote against de Gaulle in the referendum. He then held a senior position at NATO where he had become convinced that Communist cells were at work in Algeria. General Zeller, a former Chief of Army Staff, and General Jouhaud, a former Chief of Air Staff, were both retired officers.

Generals Challe and Zeller, accompanied by Colonel Broizat, a former paratroop commander, arrived secretly in Algiers on the 20th, in an aircraft made available to them by General Nicot, the acting Chief of the French Air Staff, and General Bigot, commanding the French air force in Algeria. General Gardy, a former Inspector-General of the Foreign Legion, also retired, and also one of the plotters, reached Algeria secretly about the same time. Predominant in the plotting were four colonels who were still on the active list. These were Colonels Lachroy (a former head of the 5th Bureau), Gardes (also a former head of the 5th Bureau, who had been tried and acquitted for his part in the Europeans' Revolt of January 1960), Godard (a former head of the security services in Algeria), and Argoud (a former Chief of Staff of the Algiers Army Corps).

On the 21st, rumours of military unrest reached General Gambiez, the Commander-in-Chief in Algeria; for example, a suspicious approach to a junior officer was reported to him by General Simon, commanding in Tizi-Ouzou. Gambiez passed these on to Morin, the Delegate-General, who informed the Government in Paris that evening by telephone. In the late evening, further reports reached General Gambiez, this time of unauthorized troop movements, especially from the direction of the army camps at Zeralda, about 30 miles from Algiers. Accompanied by General Saint-Hillier, the commander of the 10th Paratroop Division, Gambiez set out by car to investigate, meeting on the way a Foreign Legion convoy heading for Algiers, which would neither stop nor obey the Generals' orders. The Generals could only turn round and follow this convoy into Algiers.

The Foreign Legion convoy was in fact the spearhead of the revolt and consisted of paratroops of the 1st Foreign Legion Paratroop Regiment. They reached Algiers about 2 a.m. (22nd); immediately surrounding Government House, where the Delegate-General Morin was, they entered and told him that Generals Challe and Zeller had taken over. As Morin was left alone for a short while, he was able to telephone the news through to Paris. A little later the rebel paratroops arrested Morin and also Buron, the French Minister of Transport, who was visiting him, as well as Generals Gambiez and Saint-Hillier. Other senior officers and officials were detained. The naval commander at Algiers, Admiral Querville, on being warned oı the approach of rebel paratroops, managed to escape from his residence and get to his naval headquarters by the sea-shore.

Silently the rebel Legion paratroops spread out through the city, seizing the radio station, the post office and other key buildings. By this time other troops, instigated by some of their officers who had been brought into the plot, moved into the revolt, and an Air Commando group from Reghala, about 15 miles from Algiers, occupied the various military headquarters in the city, while other rebel paratroops from the Blida air base seized the Prefecture and certain police stations. By dawn, the army rebels had a complete grip on Algiers. It had been an almost bloodless take-over (one French soldier had been killed in the seizure of the radio station), no armed resistance being offered to the rebels. Despite alarms and rumours, or perhaps because there had been so much talk of plots and counter-plots for so long, they had achieved complete surprise.

At 6.45 a.m. (22nd) the army rebels announced over the captured radio that the Army had taken over the country, and that Generals Challe, Jouhaud and Zeller were at the head of the movement. This was followed at 8.20 a.m. (when the radio station called itself 'Radio France' instead of 'Radio Algiers') by a statement that a state of emergency was imposed by the 'military command'. The full text of a declaration by the four generals (including Salan, who had not yet arrived) assuming full control in Algeria, was read out. At 8.45 a.m. General Challe spoke over the radio, and he was followed by General Zeller, who explained that the Army had taken over to 'preserve Algeria'. Algiers lay quiet, while the remainder of Algeria sat still, watching breathlessly to see what would happen next.

The rest of the 22nd was spent by the rebel generals in negotiations trying to persuade other generals and officers in key appointments and commands to join them. General Tridon, commanding the gendarmerie, declared for the rebels and managed to induce a few of his men to follow his lead, but generally the police quietly 'disappeared', either leaving the city or remaining out of sight. General Bigot, the Air Force commander, came out early on the side of the rebel generals, and ordered all air force personnel under his control to obey them. However, as soon as the coup had been announced, about 20 aircraft were flown by their pilots from Algerian airfields to France, and a trickle of others followed during the course of the revolt.

In Constantine the attitude of the commander, General Gouraud, was hesitant and uncertain. At 4 a.m. he had agreed to join General Challe, but later retracted.

In Oran the commander, General de Pouilly, refused to join General Challe when urged to do so by Colonel Argoud. De Pouilly decided to withdraw to Tlemcen, and Colonel Argoud was declared by the rebel generals to be the commander of the Oran region until the arrival of General Gardy. General Gardy was in the area sounding out the various Legion commanders, but he had disappointing results as they were non-committal at this stage.

In the Sahara preparations were in progress for France's fourth nuclear test, scheduled to be carried out on the 25th. The commander, General Mentre, who was in Algiers at the time, at once joined the rebel generals and ordered all his officers and soldiers to obey them.

The rebel generals had counted heavily on the support of the majority of officers holding key commands and appointments. Hardly any had been sounded out beforehand, their opinions being taken for granted, and they mostly remained passive, non-committal or hesitant. Few general officers openly declared themselves for President de Gaulle at this juncture: most said and did nothing. However, one staunch Gaullist was Admiral Querville. Colonal Godard was not able to persuade him to join the revolt, and when rebel paratroops were sent to arrest him, the Admiral escaped to a warship and steamed away to the naval base at Mers El Kebir. One general officer, who from the start of the revolt came out unequivocally and openly on the side of President de Gaulle, was General Simon, commanding at Tizi-Ouzou. A former Foreign Legion colonel and a member of the war-time Free French Forces, General Simon did much to prevent defection of officers under his command and under his influence.

During the day several units of French troops came into Algiers to join the rebels, mainly from the 25th Paratroop Division, which was in the Philippeville sector. The 14th and 18th Regiments of Chasseurs Parachutistes, and the 2nd Foreign Legion Paratroop Regiment moved into the city. Colonel Brechignac, the Chief of Staff of the 25th Paratroop Division, then ordered the remainder of the formation to move towards Algiers. The 1st Foreign Legion Armoured Regiment moved from the Constantine area to Algiers also, but elsewhere French troops, especially the conscripts, remained passively in their barracks and camps listening to the various broadcasts both from the rebels and from France on their transistor radio sets.

The Europeans in Algeria were on the whole surprised and cautious. None of the leaders had been previously contacted or sounded out by the rebel plotters. Their two principal leaders, Ortiz and Lagaillarde, were both absent in Spain; and perhaps lacking their guidance and inspiration, they were at a loss what to do. Later that day, Ortiz declared himself to be the 'Head of the Provisional Government of Algeria', but this was contemptuously ignored by the rebel generals. The Spanish authorities are reported to have assured the French Government that additional watch would be kept on these two European leaders, and also on General Salan, and that none would be allowed to leave Spain.

Colonel Godard, who was temporarily in charge of Algiers for the rebels, released a number of imprisoned Ultras, and joined by a few others they were quick to take advantage of the situation. Colonel Godard also issued weapons and ammunition from police armouries to these Ultras, most of whom were members of the so-far little known 'Organisation Armée Secrète' (Secret Army Organization), the OAS. This blossomed suddenly as the OAS was permitted by the rebels to establish a headquarters in Algiers, and a radio broadcast that evening announced that the OAS had been given the exclusive authority to issue instructions to the civilian population. The OAS forbade civilians to carry arms without its consent, or to carry out any operations on their own. Suddenly, there were hundreds of armed Europeans on the streets, wearing OAS arm-bands.

President de Gaulle had been told of the revolt just after 2 a.m., when Morin had telephoned through the initial news, and he at once put Michel Debré, his Prime Minister, in personal charge of all measures to be taken to crush it. At 6.20 a.m., the French Government issued a statement condemning the revolt, and at 1.20 p.m., Debré broadcast to the French people. General Olié was appointed Commander-in-Chief in Algeria, and all sea, air and tele-communications between Algeria and France were cut.

At 6.30 p.m. a state of emergency was declared in France, all leave for the Forces was stopped, private aircraft flights were restricted and private radio transmitters closed down by the police, who in the morning had arrested many right-wing, anti-Gaullist suspects. There were a few small demonstrations in favour of the revolt in Paris, but these came to nothing and did not engender any support from the mass of French people, who were unsympathetic to its aims. The Communists and other left-wing organizations loudly condemned the revolt, as did Ferhat Abbas, speaking from Tunis.

Meanwhile, at 9.30 a.m., Joxe, the Minister for Algeria, and General Olié left by air for Oran to assess the situation on the spot, arriving there in the afternoon.

On the second day of the revolt, two French formations were on the move, the 25th Paratroop Division from the Philippeville sector to Algiers and the 10th Paratroop Division from the Djidjelli area southwards towards Constantine. Elsewhere, French formations and units remained static and passive, the conscripts regarding events sullenly and without enthusiasm. During the course of the second morning, the remainder of the 25th Paratroop Division arrived in Algiers, when the two rebel Chasseur units were sent off to Oran to support General Gardy, who was busily engaged in trying to persuade officers to join the revolt. On General Gardy's order, the commander at Saida, General Ginestet, was arrested.

During the night Joxe and General Olié had flown from Oran to Constantine to interview the wavering General Gouraud, whom they persuaded to remain loyal to President de Gaulle. Joxe and Olié then flew back to Paris that morning (the 23rd) to report to the President. In the afternoon, the rebel general, Zeller, flew to Constantine, and was able to persuade General Gouraud, no doubt by stressing the fact that a paratroop division was marching towards the city, to join General Challe in revolt.

General Salan arrived in Algiers about 1 p.m., having managed to evade Spanish police surveillance, and as the senior rebel leader, he assumed the leading position in the revolt. The arrested Morin, the Delegate-General, General Gambiez and other senior officers and officials, were flown off to the desert oasis town of In Salah to be detained.

General Petit, after at first refusing, was personally persuaded by General Challe to join him, and was appointed rebel commander of the Algiers Army Corps, which included the city of Algiers, a job that so far had been carried out by Colonel Godard. Colonel Godard then concentrated upon helping the OAS, which was rapidly springing into vigorous life and prominence. Armed groups of the OAS openly paraded the streets, took over police stations and posts, and issued instructions to the people.

At the end of the second day the rebel generals declared that the greater part of Algeria was with them, but this was by no means true. Comparatively few senior officers had joined them, and the main body of the French officer corps was non-committal. A few medium-grade and junior officers had declared for the rebels, impelled to some extent by respect for General

Challe, who had been immensely popular, and what he stood for, and also partly (in many cases) from a sense of responsibility towards their Muslim soldiers, who they knew would obtain poor treatment should the country ever become a republic. The majority of the civilian officials would not co-operate with the rebel generals, and most had 'disappeared', as had the majority of the police.

Communications between France and Algeria remained severed, and in France there was tense watchfulness. A few plastic explosions occurred in Paris and other cities, instigated by extreme right-wing elements, but they had little effect. In fact, during the second day of the revolt, some further support for de Gaulle was received from political parties and organizations. At 8 p.m. the President broadcast, condemning the revolt and forbidding all to have anything at all to do with the rebels. He assumed special powers.

Towards evening rumours began to abound in France that the rebel generals planned an airborne invasion of Paris to depose President de Gaulle and establish a military régime. Intensive preparations were made to counter this and all airfields around the Capital were blocked and guarded. Police were concentrated in Paris, and police reserves were called out. In addition, a call was made by Debré for volunteers to assist in guarding the city against a probable paratroop landing from Algeria. Many citizens came forward for this purpose, and about 1,000 were employed on the night of the 23rd/24th to keep watch.

It was known that the rebels had sufficient transport aircraft to carry at least 1,500 troops at a time. General Nicot, the acting Chief of the French Air Staff, was almost in open sympathy with the rebels, and it is believed he had ordered his men not to fire on French aircraft. Also, there was doubt and anxiety as to how other officers, senior and junior, might react to any airborne invasion of the city. Later, at his trial, General Challe emphatically denied there was ever any plan to land paratroops in Paris, but it was most probably mooted.

On the third day of the revolt, the 24th, more defensive

measures were taken in Paris to combat anticipated invasion from the air. Military units in and around the Capital were formed into an *ad hoc* division, 90 squadrons of police reservists were recalled for duty, and about 10,000 armed police were formed into a special force to be held ready near the centre of Paris. Several senior officers in both France and Germany were either arrested or placed under 'house arrest'. General Crepin, commander of French troops in Germany, announced the loyalty of himself, his officers and soldiers to President de Gaulle. The rebel generals were formally deprived of rank and decorations.

During the day more support was received by President de Gaulle, and at 5 p.m. a token strike for one hour, as a protest against the Algerian Revolt, was called, which swelled to stupendous proportions as there was a spontaneous stoppage of work by about 10 million people in France. This indicated that a huge majority of Frenchmen were for de Gaulle and against the course of action taken by the rebel generals. However, rumours of a projected airborne invasion continued to be heavily ominous, and again that night in the Capital there was a massive 'stand-to', hundreds more civilian volunteers joining the 1,000 who had kept additional watch the previous night to supplement the police.

In Algeria, the revolt began to lose momentum and to waver as senior officers timidly came out for de Gaulle and against the rebel generals. On the second day, the 24th, no senior officer joined in the revolt. On the other hand, others spoke up for the first time; men who had been strangely quiet so far, such as General Ailleret, commanding in Bône, and General Autrand, the commander of the 25th Paratroop Division. In Constantine, the mercurial General Gouraud again changed sides, deserting the rebels, and ordering the 10th Paratroop Division, which had just arrived, back to Djidjelli. In the Sahara, General Mentre informed General Challe by telephone that he could no longer give him support.

In Oran, General Gardy had been unsuccessful in persuading the Foreign Legion Regiment at Sidi Bel Abbes to join him, and generally officers and soldiers of the Legion in Western Algeria and the Sahara would not commit themselves. General Gardy published Army plans for a unilateral cease-fire with the ALN, made by General de Pouilly, who later said that these had been compiled, together with other emergency contingency plans, by his staff in the normal way so that the French Army would be prepared for any eventuality that might arise at any time. The publication of these plans had the effect of enticing a number of French officers over to General Gardy, they thinking that the de Gaulle régime had been playing false and was about to arrange a cease-fire with the ALN in the field, preparatory to handing over the country to the FLN.

In the afternoon (24th) General de Pouilly flew from Tlemcen to have talks with General Challe, but while in Algiers was arrested by General Zeller.

The conscripts, who so far had been sullen but quiet, were immensely heartened by the token strike in France, about which they heard full details on their transistor radio sets, and in the evening they became restive. They then became reluctant to obey officers' orders, and misdirected supplies and sabotaged vehicles.

Meanwhile, the four rebel generals split responsibilities for certain governmental functions amongst themselves. General Salan became responsible for civil affairs, General Challe for military matters, General Zeller for the economy of the country, and General Jouhaud for information and propaganda. The rebel generals broadcast their intention to renew the war against the FLN, and General Challe said that his aim was 'to return a pacified Algeria to France'. That day, one of the rebel broadcasts stated that Lagaillarde had arrived in Algeria and was joining the army,[1] but a later one denied this. The four rebel generals wanted nothing to do with the Europeans' leaders, and were determined to maintain the military domination of the revolt absolute.

During the morning of the 25th, after a tense night in Paris,

---

[1] Neither Lagaillarde nor Ortiz managed to reach Algeria during the Generals' Revolt, being detained by the police in Spain.

with soldiers, police and civilian volunteers on watch, the city returned to almost normal conditions on the surface. In the course of the day more messages of support reached President de Gaulle from practically every section of the population. The token strike had started this snowball rolling and by the end of the day he was assured that the majority of the people in France were solidly behind him in this crisis—indeed most of them were openly condemning the generals' revolt out of hand. The strained state of alertness against a possible airborne invasion was maintained for the third night running. President de Gaulle broadcast, telling loyal troops to take whatever action they could against the rebels. It was announced that French units from Germany, including armoured ones, had been ordered back to Paris, and were entraining at Strasbourg, while warships had set sail for Algeria from the Toulon naval base.

In Algeria the revolt was beginning to disintegrate. More pilots escaped in their aircraft from that country to France during the day. All 'uncommitted' French officers by this time saw that the revolt had little chance of success, and one by one they declared for de Gaulle. That morning, for the first time since the coup, groups of loyal police appeared on the streets of Algiers, and by afternoon they had increased in number, but they refrained from clashing with the OAS.

The rebel generals broadcast instructions to demobilize all conscripts who had completed 18 months' service,[1] to call up eight classes of Algerian Europeans, and to re-establish the Territorial Units. This gambit was designed to induce Europeans to be sympathetic to the revolt, and to give some encouragement to the recalcitrant conscripts that they might soon be sent home again.

During the 25th, support in Algeria for the rebel generals began to fall away, slowly at first and then with increasing speed. In the morning the radio station at Constantine, for example, did not relay the rebel broadcasts from Algiers, and

---

[1] The normal legal term for a French conscript was 18 months, but most had to serve for about 27 months.

in the evening this station announced that 'legality' had been restored.

In Oran, General Gardy was not doing so well, having failed to win over Admiral Querville, who with the ships under his command at Oran and Mers El Kebir remained a serious obstacle to the success of the revolt. In an attempt to force the issue, General Gardy used rebel paratroops to try and influence the situation, but they withdrew after the ships fired warning shots at them. General Gardy then left Oran. Joxe and General Olié had returned to Mers El Kebir, and were waiting to step in and take action when the revolt failed.

Seeing that the majority of the Army officers in Algeria were against him, and that what little support he had gained was being lost, General Challe decided in the late afternoon to surrender, and thus bring the abortive revolt to an end before French blood was spilt. Open signs of the failure were to be seen during the evening. Rebel paratroops were withdrawn towards Government House, and as they evacuated sectors of the city, their places were taken by the reappearing police, who returned to their stations and took over the posts that had been used by the OAS. On several occasions shots were exchanged between rebel troops and the police. At 11.30 p.m., the Algiers radio station was again in loyal hands.

The generals' revolt collapsed suddenly, and at 1.50 a.m. (26th), General Challe surrendered and was taken away to Zeralda camp, to be flown to Paris for trial. Rebel troops also surrendered and were put into trucks to be taken back to their camps under arrest. Generals Salan, Jouhaud, Zeller and Gardy 'disappeared', as did many officers who had taken prominent parts in the revolt.

On the 26th, Delegate-General Morin, General Gambiez, the Commander-in-Chief, and other detained senior officers and officials were brought back from In Salah to resume their former posts. Both Joxe and General Olié arrived in Algiers, and the task of restoring order and arresting disloyal officers began. Detachments of naval and marine personnel were drafted into Algiers to help.

During the 26th and 27th, Generals Gouraud, Bigot, Petit and Mentre were arrested, and on 6th May, General Zeller surrendered after being in hiding. On 28th April it was announced that the 1st Foreign Legion Paratroop Regiment, the 14th and 18th Regiments of Chasseurs Parachutises and the Air Commando were to be disbanded. Many officers of these regiments were arrested. All recruiting for the Foreign Legion was suspended, and for a time the fate of the Legion itself was in doubt.

In all about 40,000 officers and men had been involved in the revolt or had come out openly on the side of the rebel generals, at least for a time, and a witch hunt took place to weed out the major culprits; in it regular soldiers denounced conscripts, seniors their juniors, and vice versa. By the 29th, over 5 generals and 200 officers had been arrested, and about 160 civilians, mainly members of the OAS, were taken into custody. A number of civilians were peremptorily expelled to France. Further arrests of army officers went on for several days, until President de Gaulle ordered a halt, lest the whole structure of the Army be irreparably damaged.

A large number of weapons had been handed out from police armouries to members of the OAS, and about 8,000 were handed back, or recovered in the subsequent police searches. By 30th April, it was stated that about 4,500 arms, including about 300 sub-machine-guns, were still unaccounted for. The police estimated that there were between 15,000 and 20,000 arms of various sorts secretly in the hands of the Europeans in Algeria. All Algerian newspapers were suspended from publication until further notice.

In May, a special tribunal was set up to try senior officers involved in the generals' revolt, and sentenced Challe and Zeller each to 15 years' imprisonment, while Salan, Jouhaud and half a dozen others were sentenced to death *in absentia*. Another similar tribunal was established to try less senior officers, who were variously imprisoned, given suspended sentences, removed from the service or transferred. Over 200 officers,[1] for example,

[1] This number soon rose to 600.

were dismissed from the Army without any pension rights, and many others were abruptly retired. The comparatively light sentences on Challe and Zeller were perhaps because of the almost total lack of bloodshed in the revolt. The only shots fired against the rebels with hostile intent were from naval guns.

The generals' revolt had begun with a rush of success, but it quickly lost momentum, wavered and then abruptly fizzled out. The main reasons for its failure can be said to be lack of general support from the army officers and the Europeans, reluctance of civilian officials and police to co-operate, the hesitation of senior officers, the absence of a 'second phase' to the plan, no external support, the lack of a parallel movement in France to complement it, and transistor radios.

The chief planner, the efficient General Challe, had clearly over-estimated his personal popularity and influence. Retired officers, no matter how well they had done when serving, have little appeal to ambitious regular officers, and are accordingly regarded with a degree of suspicion. Their links, power and patronage were severed when they left the Army and went on the retired list. There were also hurt feelings on the part of senior officers who were not consulted beforehand, which retarded fuller co-operation.

The revolt was a completely military plot, and notorious European leaders, such as Ortiz and Lagaillarde, were neither consulted or informed, nor their presence wanted at all, a factor that did much to deter the Europeans from rallying to the army rebels. The Ultra organization, the OAS, was barely established at this period and little known, and did not yet have full approval from the Europeans.

Civilian officials had been at loggerheads with the Army for some time, as the Army thoughtlessly undid much of the progressive work and usurped many civilian functions, so they were not attracted to the idea of a military junta in power in Algeria, or in France. There had always been a degree of friction and suspicion between the police and the Army in Algeria, and the fact that the police were under a military commander was not popular with them. Co-operation could hardly be expected to be spontaneous and enthusiastic in the circumstances.

The absence of a 'second phase' to the plan of revolt was a significant omission, and indicated that far too much reliance had been placed on anticipated support from all sections of the French people, both in Algeria and France, to unseat President de Gaulle. The plan, sound enough in its initial stages as far as it went from a purely military point of view, abruptly hung poised, breathless and uncertain. The rebel generals did not know what to do next. Poised on one foot, they did not know where to place the other one to make the next step forward. They had to 'play it off the cuff', which they were not able to do so well. There was a distinct lack of foresight in planning, and hardly any political acumen.

No movement of revolt such as this one could have hoped to have succeeded in its aims (which presumably were to secure the removal of President de Gaulle and to substitute other leaders, or a military junta, with a stronger policy for a French-Algeria) without the support, or even the leadership, of a parallel combined political-military-civilian movement in Paris, where French political power lay. There was none. The rebel generals and the fellow plotters had been sadly misinformed over French opinion. French people as a whole cared less about Algeria, the Europeans and the French regular officers fighting there, than they ever suspected. Most families in France simply wanted their conscript sons back home. The honour of the French Army meant little to them, and the Europeans in Algeria, with whom they had hardly anything in common, less.

The French Army—meaning in this instance the cadre of regular officers, which had through circumstances assumed an almost autonomous position in Algeria—had over-estimated its popularity, political ability and influence. In the days of the Fourth Republic, and its succession of weak prime ministers, this revolt might possibly have succeeded. But de Gaulle was a statesman of a different calibre. The Army became suddenly aware that it was unpopular and that its policy for a French-Algeria had little appeal to the average Frenchman.

General Challe, who had also been popular with the Americans when at his NATO post, optimistically hoped that America might aid the revolt, or at the very least take up a neutral position over it. It was well known that America was not pleased at the independent line President de Gaulle was taking in NATO and European policy generally, and would not have been averse to more amenable leadership in France. Challe had anticipated at least moral support from the USA, and at one stage of the revolt had sent a message to the American Consulate in Algiers asking for help, but this had been bluntly refused. It is true that only belatedly did President Kennedy declare for de Gaulle and openly condemn the rebel generals. Also, there was no doubt that the American Central Intelligence Agency was actively involved in, and had knowledge of, some aspects of the planning and preparation, and perhaps also of the revolt itself, but nowadays this is firmly discounted. This is mentioned to show that there might have been sound reasons for Challe expecting American aid that was not forthcoming.

An elementary military mistake, that may not be obvious to everyone, had been to use Foreign Legion troops as the spearhead of the revolt, and to keep them in such a dominant position throughout. Foreign Legion soldiers, so well known and admired in other countries, were not always so popular in France, or with the French Army. Some French officers tended to suspect or dislike the Legion.

Yet another factor that contributed in no small measure to the collapse of the revolt, and one that one day may have far-reaching effects in all types of war in the future, was the transistor radio set, which was possessed, and listened to attentively, by so many of the French conscripts. This enabled them to hear Government broadcasts from France and to compare them with statements and announcements given out over the rebel radio stations. When President de Gaulle told them to obstruct the rebels in every way they could, there was a reaction of widespread movement of disobedience and sabotage of the revolt. Through the medium of their transistor radio sets, the conscripts were able to feel the pulse of the French nation, and to know how the people were reacting and how they were thinking. The transistor radio set made all the difference between ignorant, bewildered sheep, and well-informed citizens.

The collapse of the generals' revolt was greeted with satisfaction by all factions, parties and groups in France and Algeria, except those of the extreme right wing or those supporting a French-Algeria, but there was criticism of the Government's handling of the situation.

CHAPTER 11

The Final Phase
April 1961 — July 1962

No major French actions were mounted during the final phase of the war, although there were plenty of minor punitive ones. Likewise, the ALN essayed no large operations but instead made its presence felt by occasional, vicious guerilla tactics. A sort of uneasy military stalemate set in, with the ALN concentrating on survival, politics and terrorism — in that order. Outside Algeria, the FLN placed emphasis on political intrigue, bargaining and the manipulation of world opinion. The final phase was blackened by a spate of OAS terrorism and destruction, which led to French soldiers firing on 'Frenchmen'. Protracted negotiations preceded the total eclipse of the Europeans in Algeria and the success of the insurgent cause.

When the Generals' Revolt collapsed, the Europeans in Algeria saw a bleak future ahead of them, and in final desperation many Ultras joined and supported the OAS, which quickly swelled in numbers as its tentacles dug firmly into European communities in most cities and towns of the country. Ex-General Salan assumed the leadership of this organization, with ex-General Jouhaud as his deputy, and he was joined by many other officers implicated in the recent revolt who, evading arrest, had gone underground — such as ex-General Gardy and ex-Colonels Godard, Broizat, Lacheroy, Gardes and others — which gave it the predominant character of an underground militant force. The OAS divided the country up into three zones, Algiers, Bône and Oran, and a military pattern command structure and administrative framework were established.

OAS leaders were not all military, and there were a few prominent Ultras, such as Susini, who had a big say in policy and direction. These civilian leaders were relied upon to recruit personnel into the OAS and to indoctrinate them. They were also relied upon to rally the Europeans and to persuade them to give full support.

The strategy of the OAS, based on psychological and subversive warfare principles, was hammered out by the group of ex-colonels, several of whom had considerable experience in this field, both in Indo-China and Algeria. The OAS leaders believed that a revolutionary movement, given enough popular support, could dislocate established authority and gain its overthrow by terrorism, sabotage and mass demonstrations. Accordingly, the OAS formed its own terrorist, psychological and political sections, modelled largely on the FLN pattern, to achieve its purpose, which was to make normal government completely impossible for the President's Delegate-General in Algeria. It does not seem to have looked further forward than that step.

There was a difference of opinion in the OAS between the military and civilian elements over policy, aims and ideology. Being single-minded, the military leaders wanted, first and foremost, to overthrow President de Gaulle, while the civilians wanted as the main priority to defend the interests of the Europeans in Algeria, of whom a proportion were openly prepared to settle for partition, although there was no doubt the majority wanted an absolute French-Algeria most of all. Ex-General Salan met continual difficulties through the opposition of civilian OAS leaders to his policies and plans.

OAS commandos were recruited, mainly, from Foreign Legion deserters, young Ultras from the poorer quarters of the cities, and a few Muslims. All were paid[1] and became professional terrorists. Many ruthless ALN methods and terrorist stratagems were adopted. The OAS had seized large sums of money from Government safes during the Generals' Revolt, and it also began to make a small levy on Europeans, which

[1] At first it was the equivalent of about £36 a month.

quickly became a large one. Arms and ammunition had been obtained in the Generals' Revolt, more were stolen or fraudulently obtained. Efforts were made to buy weapons abroad.

OAS terrorism was directed mainly against Government supporters and members of the police and armed forces engaged in combating it. Starting with an average of 14 terrorist acts a day, this figure rose to about 31 daily by the end of the year. In the month of May, for example, there were 222 plastic bomb attacks, while in June there were 229. A notable incident was the murder in Algiers, on 31st May, by the OAS of the police chief. The use of plastic explosives was confined to the OAS terrorists, who became known as 'plastiqueurs', but they also indiscriminately threw bombs into crowds and cafés, as did Muslim terrorists. In Oran, where ex-General Gardy had taken command of the OAS, terrorist acts, which had been comparatively few before May 1961, sharply increased.

Parallel with the rise of OAS terrorism was that of Muslim terrorism, especially by the underground ALN organization, which mainly directed its attacks against Muslim collaborators with the French. Muslim Gaullists suffered from both groups, and often it was not possible to determine which was responsible for what. In addition, to add to this confusion, the MNA terrorist organization suddenly became active in Algeria, and selected FLN personalities for its targets.

This heavy increase in terrorism generated communal mob violence. When Europeans were the victims, other Europeans became excited and bitter and so were easily provoked into taking instant reprisals on Muslims. A similar reaction occurred when Muslims were the victims of bomb attacks or shootings. This fear and hate led to the gradual segregation of the Muslim and European communities, actively assisted by both the FLN and the OAS. Mass demonstrations, encouraged by both organizations, also tended to end in racial violence.

On 8th May, President de Gaulle broadcast to the nation reaffirming his Algerian policy, which was unequivocally one of self-determination. Secret exchanges were resumed between the

French and the Provisional Algerian Governments, and it was tentatively arranged that the projected Evian Talks (which had fallen through in April because Joxe, the Minister for Algerian Affairs, had said he would also negotiate with the MNA) should commence on the 11th. But there was some delay, and it was not until the following day that Joxe announced discussions would open at Evian on the 20th. A simultaneous announcement was made by the FLN from Tunis.

Just previously, on the 19th, Ferhat Abbas affirmed the FLN desire for peace and to maintain friendly relations with France after independence.

At Evian, the FLN delegation, which stayed on the Swiss side of Lake Geneva and was flown over daily by helicopter, was headed by Belkacem Krim, the Deputy Prime Minister and Foreign Minister in the Provincial Algerian Government, while the French delegation was led by Joxe. Belkacem Krim was considered to be a hopeful choice, as although he was an 'historic' leader of the rebellion and an ex-Wilaya commander, he was known to favour negotiations rather than a resumption of war.

Immediately, there arose differences over the Sahara, which the FLN insisted was part of Algeria, and the French said was a separate question. After a brief adjournment, the Evian Talks were resumed on the 23rd, it being agreed not to publish details currently of the negotiations. Talks were to be held on alternate days to enable delegations to consult their respective governments.

Seeming vaguely and momentarily to favour partition, President de Gaulle said on 29th June that if peace talks were unsuccessful the European population could be grouped around Algiers and Oran, as it might be easier to defend two departments than 13. The mere suggestion that partition might be a solution caused the FLN to call a general strike—which was total in Algiers, and generally successful elsewhere—and to arouse Muslim demonstrations that ended in 88 Muslim dead. On 12th July, de Gaulle back-pedalled, broadcasting that the French accepted the fact that Algeria should be an entirely independent state, and was ready to organize free self-determination with the FLN leaders.

Talks then seemed to progress better, the delegates moving to the Château de Lugrin, outside Evian, when discussions became known as the 'Lugrin Talks', but these broke down on 28th July over the Sahara problem, and were adjourned indefinitely.

A pause followed until 5th September, when President de Gaulle said at a press conference that France might recognize Algerian sovereignty over the Sahara, which, although flatly contradicting the conditions laid down by Joxe, broke the deadlock. Two weeks later the Provisional Algerian Government indicated its willingness to reopen negotiations. On 2nd October, de Gaulle said very much the same thing. Nothing positive immediately emerged from these public exchanges, although secret contacts were maintained and feelers put out by both sides.

Meanwhile, on 6th August, the CNRA (the National Council of Algerian Revolution) met in Tripoli, and at the conclusion of the session on the 27th changes were announced in the Provisional Algerian Government, the main one being the replacement of Ferhat Abbas as Prime Minister by Ben Khedda. As Ben Khedda had known left-wing sympathies, this seemed to indicate that the revolutionary socialist members had regained influence and that the Council as a whole wished to pursue a firmer line, thus reversing the moderate trends brought into prominence in the January 1960 reshuffle.

Ferhat Abbas was probably dropped because he was ill and tired[1] and perhaps because of the immense personal popularity he had gained amongst the Muslims inside Algeria, which threatened to upset the 'collective leadership' principle. Again, he may have been considered too moderate for the hard negotiations ahead. After the failure of the Battle of Algiers in 1957, Ben Khedda had lost influence with the FLN, but now he seemed once again to be in the ascendant. Already, within the

[1] Ferhat Abbas had never fully recovered from a road accident in Morocco in 1959.

FLN leadership there were powerful rivalries that were only with difficulty kept within bounds and concealed from the public gaze.

To enable a better climate for negotiations to be obtained, several measures were taken by the French, and on the 20th, the day the Evian Talks began, all French armed forces in Algeria were ordered to cease aggressive operations and not to take action against the ALN unless in self-defence or in pursuit of persons committing acts of terrorism. The Delegate-General, Morin,[1] said this was not a 'cease-fire' but a unilateral breaking off offensive actions, which would apply throughout the whole of Algeria and the Sahara, except in zones up to 30 kilometres from the frontiers, where the French Army would continue to effectively bar efforts to reinforce the ALN from either Tunisia or Morocco. The Commander-in-Chief, General Gambiez, said firmly that any attempt to cross frontiers and attack in force would be regarded as a breach of the truce. There was, however, plenty of minor, spasmodic activity in the country, and there were several small attempts to break through the frontier barriers. Generally, the trend was that there were fewer incidents in the countryside, but more in the cities and towns.

Morin was instructed to step up the release of certain prisoners and internees, and by 16th June he was able to announce that since 20th May 6,200 had been released. Three of the kidnapped FLN leaders (the other two were in hospital at the time) were allowed more comfortable confinement conditions. The policy was no longer to forcibly regroup Algerian Muslims.

As the ALN inside Algeria had almost ceased to fight the French Army anyway, the FLN leaders became deeply concerned lest, should negotiations fail, it take to politics and banditry and thus no longer remain an effective fighting force. The FLN decided to do all possible to improve the discipline of the ALN outside the country, now a body of some 35,000 fairly

---

[1] Other details of interest given by Morin were that on this day (the 20th) 4,500 'rebels' captured in arms were in military internment centres and 12,000 civilians, including some 270 Europeans, were detained as well.

well armed and trained men, under Colonel Boumedienne, the nominated Chief of Staff. This external ALN force, loyal to the CNRA, would be available to move into Algeria, when independence was achieved, to establish the authority of the Provisional Algerian Government, to keep order and enforce decisions on the almost openly intractable and non-co-operative Wilaya commanders and fighters in the interior.

In a statement on 6th June, Pierre Mesmer, Minister for the Armed Forces, explained to the French Army reasons for the cessation of offensive action in Algeria, saying that while the ALN was beaten in the field and only a few scattered armed bands remained, the FLN remained a powerful diplomatic, political and sentimental influence that could not be ignored. Referring to an incident that happened on 20th May, when an Algerian Muslim garrison deserted with its arms, killing its French officers, he insisted that 'France would not abandon her children'.

An increased effort had been made throughout Algeria by the ALN to induce the Algerian Muslim Harkis to desert, but despite all endeavours comparatively few defected, as the hard core was loyal to the French, perhaps out of sheer necessity. There were about 400 Algerian Muslim officers in the French military service, and in July a regulation removed the bar from their achieving general-rank. In October, Colonel Rafa, an Algerian Muslim, was promoted brigadier-general, the first Muslim to reach this height, but he was not given an active command.

On 7th June, General Ailleret was appointed 'High Commander of the Forces in Algeria' (Commandant Supérieur des Forces Interarmées), in place of General Gambiez, the Commander-in-Chief, who was given another post in France. At the same time other changes were made amongst senior commanders and officers. In July, a division was transferred from Algeria to Germany, and it was announced that another would soon be withdrawn, together with air force elements that included jet aircraft. It was not until 29th December that President de Gaulle said the major part of the French Army would be regrouped in Europe in 1962, when, in fact, this movement was already under way.

Generally, the Army in Algeria was regarded as highly suspect by the French Government, and rations, ammunition and vehicle fuel were doled out to it in small, restricted amounts. Out of approximately 10,000 regular French officers serving in Algeria, a few had been dismissed or resigned since April 1961. Many were suspected of having taken a secret oath not to accept Algerian independence, but de Gaulle heavily counted on the French Army to be swayed by the mass of conscript opinion to remain loyal to the Government and to take action against the OAS whenever ordered to do so. Salan, on the other hand, gambled that a large section of the Army would either join, or actively sympathize with, the OAS. He certainly hoped that all, regular and conscript alike, retained the old taboo that Frenchmen would never fire on Frenchmen.

By August 1961 it was thought that the OAS had about 15,000 armed, active members, and there were strong detachments in Oran, Bône and Constantine, beside the major group in Algiers. More arms had been smuggled in from Spain, and plastic explosives were bought, stolen or obtained by trickery, such as wearing French Army uniforms to gain entry into French arms depots. This made the OAS, now better organized, more ambitious. From assassinations of pro-Government officials, including some army officers, its efforts were turned to provoking communal riots. According to the tenor of President de Gaulle's broadcasts on Algeria, and in the intervals when negotiations between French and Provisional Algerian Governments lapsed, throughout the remainder of 1961 there was a series of alternatively FLN- or OAS-provoked demonstrations that inevitably led to damage, violence and loss of life. During the last quarter of the year, for example, it was estimated that some 60 people were killed by the OAS and some 70 wounded.

Already on 21st September, Radio Algiers had been forcibly interrupted by the emboldened OAS and broadcasts made by both Salan and Gardy. Then for a few days an OAS clandestine radio station operated in the city, issuing instructions to the

Europeans, until it was discovered and closed down by the police. It was in September that the OAS made an attempt, in France, on the life of President de Gaulle. During November the OAS made determined efforts to establish itself in Metropolitan France.

Squads of armed police were formed to combat the OAS by taking ruthless action and employing special methods, and the members became popularly known as 'Barbuses' (bearded ones). Recognizing the danger, the OAS commandos hit back whenever they could, and during the last two months of the year there were several clashes between the two. On 29th January (1962) OAS commandos blew up a villa on the outskirts of Algiers used as a headquarters by the Barbuses, in which it is believed that at least 18 policemen were killed. The following month the OAS were employing bazookas in attacks on the special police squads.

In January there was an intensification of terrorism, and the OAS seemed to dominate Algiers, ordering strikes and demonstrations as it took a firm hold on the Europeans by a mixture of fear and sympathy. The OAS boldly issued proclamations, stuck up posters and daubed slogans on walls and buildings everywhere. It ordered Europeans to hoard food, to withdraw their savings from banks and gave them mobilization instructions. In the first month of the year it was estimated that 220 Europeans and 355 Muslims were killed, and 382 Europeans and 608 Muslims were wounded, by either the OAS, ALN or the MNA terrorist elements.

At first the FLN had no interest in the OAS, saying that it was an affair between Frenchmen, but as OAS terror squads indiscriminately murdered so many Muslims the FLN ordered its ALN underground units into retaliatory action. The ALN had really stopped fighting the French Army, and in Algiers, as elsewhere, had concentrated largely on political activities. ALN terror squads were formed and many Europeans were killed or kidnapped by them. Other armed ALN detachments had to be used to protect Muslim cafés and buildings from OAS action. February was a bad month, and so was March. Perhaps the blackest day was 28th March, when 65 people were killed and 93 wounded in Algeria. The constant aim of the OAS was to provoke communal riots on such a scale that the French Army would have to intervene—on the side of the Europeans it was naturally anticipated—and so make a cease-fire with the ALN impossible. For example, an OAS attempt was made to raise insurrection in Orléansville.

The secret contacts between the French and the Muslims had setbacks, such as on 2nd November, when Ben Bella and other detained FLN leaders led a hunger strike that eventually involved over 4,000 Muslim prisoners. This did not end until the 20th, when secret exchanges were resumed in both Rome and Geneva, continuing in an uncertain fashion throughout January (1962) and February. They did, nevertheless, progress and secret talks were held at ministerial level at Les Rousses, in the Jura near the Swiss border, from the 11th until the 18th of February.

Next, when the CNRA met in Tripoli between the 22nd and the 27th of February, it empowered its delegation to conclude agreements without further reference back to it. This showed how close the end was, and what turned out to be the final round of negotiations began at Evian on 7th March. They ended on the 18th, with a cease-fire agreement and a general declaration of future Algerian policy, signed by both Joxe and Belkacem Krim.

A Provisional Executive was to be set up, the rights of Europeans were to be guaranteed, French military forces were to withdraw within three years, the French were to lease Mers El Kebir, and would be able to use other installations in both Algeria and the Sahara for a period. The FLN promised to cooperate on the hand-over of power, and to take no discriminatory action against the Muslim Harkis[1] who had served France so faithfully. Those were the principal conditions; there were others.

---

[1] This was not honoured, and after independence it is thought that many were killed, often after ill-treatment, while others were detained or put to forced labour. Several thousand emigrated to France for security.

At noon on 19th March 1962 the cease-fire came into effect, and a Cease-Fire Commission, consisting of five Frenchmen and five members of the FLN, held its first meeting on 6th April. The ALN units in Algeria were to remain in their camps or to stay in certain defined areas. This was adhered to, and on the whole where ALN discipline remained there were no incidents, but where it had fallen apart there were incidents of banditry against European farmers, mainly by the younger Muslim elements who however had no political motive.

The previous day, the 18th, Ben Bella and other captured FLN leaders were released from detention and flown to Evian to take part in the final sessions of the talks. On the 20th, they flew to Morocco to take the salute at the insurgent ALN's first public parade, at an army camp near Oudjda, when about 1,200 ALN soldiers marched past.

On the 19th, the post of Delegate-General ceased to exist and in its place Christian Fouchet was appointed High Commissioner. On the 23rd, the French Government issued a decree granting a wide amnesty for offences committed during the course of the war.[1] On the 27th, Abda Rahman Farés, a former President of the Algerian Assembly, was released from detention and he agreed to become President of the interim Provisional Executive. A signatory of the 'Manifesto of 121', and long an active Muslim politician, he had been intermediary for President de Gaulle after his 'Peace of the Brave' offer, but was suspected by the French of being responsible for its failure and thus placed in detention. The next day, the 28th, the Provisional Executive was formed, consisting of six members of the FLN, three other Muslims and three Europeans, and it was formally installed on 7th April, at Rocher-Noir, about 40 miles from Algiers.

On 8th April, a referendum was held in Metropolitan France on the 'March 19th proposals',[2] as they were known,

[1] Messali Hadj was not released from his residential restrictions until 28th May.
[2] The referendum read: 'Do you wish Algeria to become an independent state co-operating with France under the conditions laid down by the declaration of 19th March 1962?'

and they were approved by a 90 per cent vote in favour.

On 19th March, the FLN had called off terrorism; the OAS on the other hand intensified it, trying to provoke the Muslim population into communal riots. But the FLN kept a firm grip on the people and so massive retaliation was avoided. Driven to desperation by events, the OAS resorted to even more extreme measures. Already, on 18th March, it had set up a National Council of French Resistance, with ex-General Salan nominated as Commander-in-Chief, to form a Provisional Government, and military courts were established by the OAS to try Muslims caught looting or committing other offences.

On 20th March, mortar bombs were fired into the Casbah by members of the OAS. Also, six French soldiers were shot and killed in a military truck that would not stop when they ordered it to do so. This caused the Army and the police to mount a huge clearing operation in the Bab El Ouad district of Algiers, an OAS stronghold, which was first cordoned off. Hard fighting followed as OAS members stood fast in pill-boxes and houses, firing back at the troops and police. Six days later, when all OAS elements had been rooted out, the cost was found to be 15 soldiers and police killed, and 71 wounded, while the OAS lost at least 20 dead and over 80 wounded, and more than 3,000 were arrested.

This battle marked the vital change of emphasis on the part of the Army, which had by this time most decidedly turned against the OAS, and was prepared to shoot and kill 'Frenchmen' if necessary. President de Gaulle had ordered that the OAS insurrection be broken by 'all means', and the Army rallied to him. There was no longer any doubt as to whether the bulk of the Army would disobey orders to take action against the Europeans. This new, tough attitude on the part of most army officers, as well as practically all the conscripts, resulted in more ruthless measures being taken, and more exacting searches made, replacing the former rather weak and perfunctory ones.

In Oran, the OAS set up barricades, and fought back whenever the Army and police tried to remove them. However, the backbone went out of this aggressive resistance on 25th March, when, during a search for a clandestine OAS radio, ex-General Jouhaud was arrested. He had been in charge of the Oran area since August (1961) when Gardy had been appointed deputy commander of the OAS.

A month later (on 20th April), ex-General Salan was arrested in Algiers, when the command of that organization was assumed by Gardy. The removal of Salan stripped the OAS of the last vestige of respectability.

The OAS sternly ordered all Europeans, under penalty of death, to stay where they were, but despite a few summary executions, they were leaving the country in ever-increasing numbers. Faced with the bleak choice of either the 'suitcase or the coffin', they realized that the end, and not a very satisfactory one for them, was in sight. By the following month, hundreds were leaving Algeria daily.

A number of armed groups of the MNA, varying in size and active potential, still survived scattered at odd places across Algeria, and the OAS made efforts to enlist their support in the fight against the ALN, to the extent of issuing them with arms and ammunition on the condition they were used against other Muslim insurgents. Some co-operation existed for a short while but this suddenly came to an end on 23rd May, when an agreement was made between the FLN and the MNA not to fight each other.

Early in May, the OAS adopted a scorched earth policy so that little of value would be left for a Muslim government to take over, and many schools, public buildings and similar places were burnt. Violence continued, and 2nd May, for example, was a particularly bad day, when some 100 people were killed in Algiers. But gradually the Army and the police were able to enforce stricter measures against the OAS groups, and this tended to curb their terrorist activities. In France, where the OAS had obtained a tenuous foothold, the police were winning the battle against this organization, although there were attempts to assassinate President de Gaulle and other prominent figures.

THE FINAL PHASE

About this time many Europeans, the majority active members of the OAS, were kidnapped by the Muslim anti-OAS squads as a retaliatory measure. It was estimated that about 606 were seized by the ALN between 19th March and 24th June, of whom about 157 were released fairly soon after capture.

The first step to ending OAS terrorism occurred on 18th May, when a secret approach was made to the Provisional Executive by prominent civilian OAS leaders, indicating that the OAS was prepared to accept Algerian independence if new guarantees were given to the European community. Further contacts of this nature caused the OAS to issue leaflets ordering the suspension of terrorist activities. This was repeated in a broadcast, and on 31st May, OAS terrorism virtually ceased.

Negotiations were begun between the OAS and the Provisional Executive on 1st June, but these broke down on the 5th, as the OAS demanded to be recognized as representative of all Europeans living in the country, while the FLN insisted that there was no place for a racial party in the new Algeria.

On the 7th, the OAS resumed destruction of public buildings and committed other acts of terrorism, but two days later (9th) it instructed its members to cease making attacks on people and to limit their activities to material destruction alone.

Negotiations were resumed on the 13th and 14th, but no progress was apparent until the 17th, when the OAS, suddenly accepting the terms offered by the FLN, called off all terrorist activity. This agreement was repudiated by OAS elements in both Oran and Bône, where there was a last-minute wave of destruction, as well as in parts of Algiers, but Colonel Dufour, who had become the chief OAS negotiator, firmly ordered the OAS to cease fire on 26th June. This order was generally obeyed, although there were a few isolated incidents afterwards. On the 27th, ex-General Gardy with other military and civilian leaders of the OAS, after a last clandestine broadcast in which he said that the struggle had become hopeless and that 'Algeria was dead', fled the country. This was virtually the end of the war.

As it drew to a close there was a wave of European mass

199

emigration, it being stated that nearly 300,000 had left the country since 1st May, and that many were leaving every day.[1]

Although Algiers swarmed with hundreds of OAS personnel and sympathizers, bitterly chagrined Ultras, Foreign Legion deserters and criminals, the curfew was lifted on the 30th, in time for the referendum to be held the next day, 1st July. Susini of the OAS made a broadcast urging Europeans to vote in favour of it, and (out of a 91 per cent poll) 97 per cent did so.

President de Gaulle announced the results on the 3rd, when Fouchet, the French High Commissioner, formally handed over sovereign power to the Provisional Executive. That afternoon, Ben Khedda and other ministers of the Provisional Algerian Government arrived in Algiers. That day the newly independent state was recognized by Britain, America, the Soviet Union, Red China and other countries. On 8th October, Algeria became a member of the United Nations.

A few brief figures may give an indication of the cost in human lives and suffering of this $7\frac{1}{2}$-year-long insurgent war in Algeria. Its magnitude in this respect is often overlooked. For example, the 42,090 acts of terrorism recorded caused civilian casualties to the numbers of 10,704 European (2,788 killed, 7,541 wounded and 375 missing), and 43,284 Muslim (16,378 killed, 13,610 wounded and 13,296 missing). Over and above this, in France alone the total estimated numbers of Algerian-Muslim victims (between 1956 and 1962) were 4,300 killed and 9,000 wounded, distributed roughly equally between the FLN and the MNA. At the time of the cease-fire (19th March) the French held about 3,600 Algerian Muslims captured in action in five military internment camps, and about 14,000 other Muslim internees elsewhere. At least 1·8 million Algerian Muslims were uprooted from their homes, or were forced to leave them because of the fighting.

It was estimated that the ALN in the course of the whole war lost at least 141,000 men killed. The number of wounded can only be vaguely guessed at.

---

[1] By November 1962, it was estimated that only about 150,000 Europeans remained in Algeria, out of approximately one million, a year previously.

The French also suffered comparatively heavy losses, which were stated to amount to 12,000 regular French troops (being about 9,000 Frenchmen, 1,500 Legionnaires and 1,500 Muslims) and 2,500 Muslim auxiliaries killed. Missing were also 198 Frenchmen.

CHAPTER 12

In Retrospect

Generally supposed to be just another example of successful insurrectionary war, on the pattern set by the Communists in Red China and French Indo-China, the Algerian War in retrospect reveals a few interesting features. Far from being a simple national movement springing from the mass of the people to throw off the French colonial yoke, it was begun by a small group of power-hungry men, shrewd, ambitious and ruthless, who had little in common with the half-starved Algerian peasant. Determined to seize control of the country, they chose the violent method of open revolt. After forming the imperative essential, a good intelligence service, they set about constructing the framework of a military organization.

A mass insurgent movement requires an ideal to inspire and cement—for example, the Communists have the sincere belief that the creed of Marx, suitably modified by the later Communist prophets and distorted to suit local conditions, is the only sound and just solution for any country's ills or problems. In the case of Algeria the ideal, or motive driving force, was that of nationalism, but this had to be discovered, polished up and then forced upon the people, who knew nothing of it. Only with difficulty had this country of diverse peoples and tribes been pacified by the French, and it had never thought of itself as a unified nation with a distinct soul of its own. Ferhat Abbas has told of how, as a young man, he searched fruitlessly for the 'Algerian nation', and came to the conclusion it had no historical basis. In short, one had to be produced to order by the revolutionaries.

The UDMA, the Ulema and the PCA, together with Ferhat Abbas and other prominent Algerian Muslim politicians, initially condemned the revolt, perhaps because they were not consulted or informed beforehand, and also perhaps because they did not understand the mechanics of insurgent warfare as well as did the CRUA. Later on, most changed their original views, either as a result of intimidation, or other forms of persuasion. The CRUA planners were fortunate in that they were able to harness the Muslim religion to help them persuade the people that there was such a thing as an Algerian nation, and then that it must become independent of France.

Overnight the CRUA became the FLN, which divided its political and military functions. The External Delegation, responsible for the political direction of the war, diplomatic contacts and procurement, moved to Cairo where it could operate openly in the security of a friendly country instead of having to hide in the mountains in the interior of Algeria, with the attendant dangers and communication problems. This was a distinct advantage, as it was able to lobby its cause freely among other nations, and try to persuade countries to sympathize actively with its struggle so as to procure money, arms and supplies for the ALN in the field. When Morocco and Tunisia became independent in 1956, it organized clandestine supply routes into Algeria, and later when funds were short obtained money from Red China. Few nations knew anything about Mao Tse-tung during the years he was forced to remain in his remote lair in Yenan — to his obvious disadvantage, as some countries might have sympathized and aided him. But the whole world knew about the Algerian Insurrection, its ideals and its needs, right from the beginning, because the External Delegation was in a position to loudly proclaim its cause.

The External Delegation was also extremely successful in putting the FLN case before the United Nations, forcing a debate on the Algerian Problem as early as September 1955, thus negating the French insistence that it was entirely a French domestic matter. When a Government-in-Exile was formed in 1958, it soon had accredited representatives in several countries, who took every opportunity to blacken the French case and to gild their own. The one big diplomatic failure was the failure to gain full support from America. Its propaganda efforts were also first class: full capital, for example, was made out of the French kidnapping of Ben Bella and other FLN leaders, and the French bombing of Sakiet.

It is true that the External Delegation lost some control over the Internal Delegation (which in effect meant the ALN in Algeria) by not attending the Soummam Conference (in August 1956), but this did not deter it from continuing to procure and send what arms and equipment it could. Later, when arms supplies were abruptly cut off and the Algerian frontiers closed more securely by the French Army, the External Delegation concentrated on building up its 'conventional' army in both the Eastern and the Western Bases, which were firmly under the political control of the Provisional Algerian Government. These 'conventional' troops were originally intended for the ultimate battle, but when it seemed that this might not be necessary, they were to be available to move into the country to enforce the Government-in-Exile's decrees when the French handed over power in Algeria. External control over the ALN inside Algeria was never absolute, owing to such factors as communication difficulties, and the individual characteristics of the Wilaya commanders and their subordinates. Thus there were in fact two separate armies, a guerilla-type one inside Algeria, and a more conventional one outside the country.

Collectively known as the Internal Delegation and initially appointed by CRUA, the Wilaya commanders were by force of circumstances autonomous in their own areas, their very survival depending upon their individual initiative and ability. Capture, death in battle and treachery decimated their ranks. Liaison between them was difficult, jealousies existed and co-operation was very poor. It was friction of this nature that led to the calling of the Soummam Conference, which introduced a measure of order and sanity.

After the Battle of Algiers in 1957, senior members of the Internal Delegation and most of the CNRA members took refuge over the Tunisian border, and others were appointed to internal commands in their stead to continue the guerilla fight against the French Army.

When the French frontier barriers became effective, blocking the bulk of arms supplies and preventing large-scale infiltration, such arms and equipment as were obtained went to the ALN contingents in the Eastern and Western Bases, where recruits could be armed and trained in safety. This caused bitter disappointment to the ALN personnel fighting inside Algeria, starved of arms and ammunition, as they saw a comparatively well-armed, inactive force sitting just across the frontiers, while they bore the brunt of the war. This led to recriminations between the two, which did not make the internal field commanders any more amenable to control by the comfortably remote External Delegation. These differences might have been exploited by the French to their own advantage to a far greater extent, as one of the main weapons of anti-subversive warfare is to find and magnify internal differences.

ALN tactics in Algeria were modelled on those of the Viet Minh in Indo-China, while its strategy was more that expounded by Mao Tse-tung. The initial terrorist outrages that signalled the outbreak of the insurrection were designed to make an impact on both the French and the Muslims, the object being surprise and seizure of the initiative from complacent and astounded French authorities.

Under cover of sporadic 'hit-and-run' tactics, employed to both impress and to seize arms and ammunition, the ALN expanded physically, spreading slowly across the northern part of the country, encountering teething troubles galore in the process. As they appeared, the small armed forces of each Wilaya undertook bold offensive guerilla tactics, but practically all suffered heavy casualties from French retaliatory action to such an extent that the insurgents had to retire hastily to less accessible parts of the country.

The ALN strategy was to establish bases in the mountains on the recommended Mao Tse-tung pattern, consolidate them and then creep and seep towards the towns and cities. In the first phase the accent was to be on the countryside and the villages, rather than on the main centres of population, and wherever the ALN gained dominance a three-man committee (consisting of a political agent, a civil affairs officer and a tax collector) was imposed on villages.

But early the cities proved to be magnets that could not be resisted by leaders in the field, and only six months after the outbreak, Algiers attracted from the mountains Belkacem Krim of Wilaya III. Other Wilaya commanders met and lingered there at times, some to their cost. Efforts were made to enlarge and improve the ALN underground in Algiers, an example copied with less success in other cities. The loss of the Battle of Algiers and the success of the French quadrillage strategy crushed the ALN and prevented them from obtaining any substantial underground hole in the population centres. Out of sheer necessity they had to concentrate upon the countryside.

The 'guerilla', or 'survival', period of the insurrection, perhaps the most vital and tricky one of all, lasted for about 20 months, during which time the infant ALN was in a disorganized muddle. The Muslim population was indifferent and uncomprehending, and became even hostile when the ALN began to levy taxes, seize food, enforce conscription and impose its views on the people. The ALN survived partly because the French authorities were slow to recognize it for what it was and so failed to deal promptly and adequately with the revolt, and partly because there was ample mountainous and under-administered terrain in which to hide.

The protracted stage of insurgent warfare could be said to have commenced after March 1956, in which month both Morocco and Tunisia became independent, enabling the ALN to form the Eastern and Western Bases. Far from graduating from the protracted stage to the mobile one—the next logical step—the ALN was forced to revert to the guerilla one in 1959. The ALN lost the long-drawn-out struggle in which strength, tenacity and weight counted, and it never reached the mobile stage at all.

Like the armies of Mao Tse-tung and Ho Chi Minh, the

ALN was a politically indoctrinated force in which political and military direction were intertwined, with politics always taking precedence. A small hard core of dedicated leaders at all levels maintained political control, command being exercised by 'three-man committees' in all units. Discipline was strict and orders had to be obeyed instantly, harsh punishments being inflicted on offenders. There was never any question of the men electing their own leaders — they were appointed, and their authority was absolute. Neither were the Communist-type public criticisms of superiors, or personal confessions of error, misdeed and politically unreliable thoughts practised as a general rule.

The initial strength of the ALN may have been in the region of 3,000, not all of whom were fighters, and during the period of survival this may have risen to 5,000. Recruiting was carried out by press-gang methods, reluctant warriors only being kept in the ranks by threats that dire reprisals would be taken on their families if they deserted.

By April 1956, as the ALN entered the protracted stage of insurgent warfare, it expanded quickly to a probable fighting strength of about 8,500, with about another 20,000 or so unarmed supporters, who were sufficient in number to enlarge and improve the intelligence and supply services. Although a few more willing volunteers came forward in this period recruiting remained a problem throughout, and the insurgents had to impose a form of conscription in areas under their control. This may help dispose of the myth that there are always many thousands of eager volunteers pressing forward to enter the ranks of an insurgent movement. The ALN policy was at first to form as large units as possible, but these proved to be unwieldy for this type of warfare, and heavy casualties were inflicted on them whenever they clashed with the French Army.

The Soummam Conference, in August 1956, affirmed collective leadership, which checked individualism or possible splintering and reduced insubordination. It introduced ranks and pay, and regularized command procedure, establishments, supporting elements and the OPA. The basic field unit was reduced in size to 350 all ranks. As the Muslim population was 'brain-washed' into supporting the FLN cause a few more volunteers came forward and there was slightly less resistance to being drafted into the ALN. The ALN then quickly rose to its probable maximum strength of about 40,000 armed and uniformed fighters, backed by some 90,000 active supporters. These numbers encouraged a trend towards larger formations, and the basic field unit rose to over 600 all ranks. Plans were laid to link units together in brigades for larger operations.

Several of the new larger units took part in the disastrous Battle for the Frontier, the only really large-scale actions of the war, in which the ALN suffered severe casualties. The French frontier barriers proved to be so formidable that the ALN was forced to give up the idea of crashing through them head-on, and fewer attempts were made to penetrate into Algeria in strength. Inside Algeria, the ALN reduced the strength of its units down to about 100 all ranks.

In 1958, two separate general staffs were set up, one in eastern and the other in western Algeria, to co-ordinate and control insurgent activity. Later, this was fused into a single general staff, operating from Tunisian territory. The FLN still thought it was necessary, under cover of a flurry of guerilla and terrorist actions, to build up a conventional army to fight an ultimate battle with the French Army, as the Viet Minh had done in Indo-China, and in the Eastern and Western Bases this idea was put into practice as arms and recruits arrived.

The implementation of the Challe Plan in 1959 severely mauled the already groggy and shaken ALN inside Algeria. This was the turning-point of the military struggle. The French Army had gained the upper hand, forcing the ALN to revert hastily to the guerilla stage of insurgent warfare. In most areas, the Challe Plan compelled the insurgents to split up into small groups of 10 or 12 for reasons of survival, and the task of the French Army remained to search them out and hunt them down. Now definitely on the defensive, the ALN in Algeria undertook fewer and fewer operations, concentrating upon survival, terrorism and political activities.

Although declared equal to men by the revolutionary leaders, the women who served in the ALN were always in a tiny minority, being used mainly as nurses, cooks and on administrative duties. If they were sufficiently educated they were employed as teachers, clerks or on political tasks. A few fought in the ranks side by side with men in battle in the early days, but this number declined as the war progressed. In the male Muslim mind a woman had a definite place and role in society and no amount of revolutionary propaganda could bend this traditional idea. Lip service was occasionally paid to the equality of women, but little more. Women had no effect on the course of the insurrection.

At the outbreak of the insurrection the ALN was extremely short of arms, and for several months this undoubtedly did much to restrict aggressive activity and retard expansion. By the end of 1955, arms became more plentiful, being smuggled in from Egypt fairly easily before the Algerian frontier barriers were established, and this enabled the expanding regular element to be given weapons. This flow from Egypt, supplemented from Iron Curtain and Western European countries as the FLN obtained funds to spend or credits, continued for almost three years, although it tended to be increasingly hampered by French naval and frontier vigilance.

The French won a huge diplomatic triumph in June 1959, when they threatened to publish lists of countries supplying arms to the FLN. This caused the ALN arms supply to dry up almost completely, to the extent that of the some 15,000 active insurgents at large inside Algeria at the end of the war, only about one-third had weapons. The ALN army outside Algeria, amounting to perhaps 25,000 men, were all armed.

Looking through rose-coloured glasses and visualizing the gay insurgent fighter materializing from thin air to strike and then disappear quickly without trace, the enthusiasts of this type of warfare too often overlook the cost in human lives and suffering this entails. Throughout the war in Algeria the insurgent casualty rate was staggeringly high, far greater (in proportion to numbers committed into action) than some of the terrible battles of World War I. For example, in the first 17 months, it is thought that the ALN lost 4,885 killed in action, a number almost equal to its fighting strength at the time.

Furthermore, in the first three years the ALN lost at least 30,000 killed and some 13,000 captured, and during the Battle of the Frontier in early 1958 it lost over 3,000 killed in action each month. These figures do not include wounded, of which no reliable figures are available, but which must, according to the laws of average as applied to battles, have been several times greater. Again, there is no mention of deserters, of whom there were many. A lesson that should be heavily underlined is that to insurgents insurgent warfare is extremely costly in human life.

The quick, unexpected attack or ambush followed by speedy withdrawal was usually a tactic of sheer necessity, the withdrawal frequently being accompanied by loss. Clashes with French troops were avoided as they tore gaps in the ranks of the ALN. Casualties, as much as any other reason, caused changes to be made in both insurgent strategy and tactics, the huge losses in action bringing the ruthless, ambitious insurgent leaders down to earth, forcing them to be more practical.

It is frequently thought that insurgent forces always have a high morale, while that of the Government forces is correspondingly low. This is another fallacy, as heavy casualties, hardships, defeats in minor skirmishes, constant movement to get away from searching troops, and shortages of arms and equipment, all combine to breed a feeling of despondency and hopelessness which only intensive indoctrination and harsh salutary punishment can counteract.

Morale in the ALN was never very high, and at times desperately low. It did begin to rise after 1956, when the people were persuaded to espouse the FLN aims, but French countermeasures in 1958 and 1959 caused morale to wane. Removal of sections of the population gave the insurgents the feeling of being cut off from the FLN, of being expendable and abandoned. By 1960 morale in the ALN in Algeria was again quite low. However, a façade of terrorist and guerilla activities was maintained, and the few major incidents were exaggerated to bolster up the spirit of the insurgents.

An ugly feature of the Algerian War was the indiscriminate use of intimidation, terror and torture by the insurgents. Completely dedicated and ruthless to the extreme, the leaders never hesitated to use these means whenever they were thought essential to a particular end, although it was admitted they were not desirable if other means could be found capable of producing the same result. Ample evidence of insurgent use of these uncivilized practices is available, and is not disputed. Later there were allegations that the French Army indulged in counterbrutalities, but investigations showed that this was not so. The only isolated instances unearthed were officially condemned. The restraint on the part of the French Army was most praiseworthy, as the temptation to retaliate in kind must at times have been overwhelming.

The first signs of European counter-terrorist activities appeared in June 1956 in the cities, and these increased spasmodically in volume as the war progressed, with the decline of the prospects and fortunes of the European community. General Massu's admitted harsh methods wrenched free the terrorist hold the FLN had fastened firmly on to the Casbah in Algiers, and this was held to be justification for any similar means used by the French Army at other times.

In both France and Algeria the gang warfare that had welled up between the FLN and the MNA was punctuated by torture and death which became commonplace as each underground organization struggled for funds, recruits and power. Intimidation and terror deterred Algerian Muslim politicians and officials from co-operating with the French authorities, and dashed President de Gaulle's hope for a third Muslim political force with which he might negotiate to the advantage of France.

In short, intimidation, terror and torture were weapons of insurgency that the FLN used to the full, but they were doubleedged ones. Another deadly insurgent warfare tactic is encouraging desertion from the opposing ranks; but men, no matter how disillusioned, bitter, hungry and weary, are not going to turn their coat unless they can be sure of fair, humane treatment. The FLN and the MNA neutralized each other's subversive desertion efforts by these very means.

Another fallacy exposed was that the Muslim masses were seething and ripe for a nationalist insurrection and desperately anxious to make any sacrifice to throw off the French Imperialist yoke. The fact was that Algeria was hardly a nation, had little pride in its nationhood, and the Muslim population was ignorant of and indifferent to the aims of the FLN. During the first 20 months they were brutally terrorized into compliance by FLN leadership, who were initially utterly indifferent to winning approbation and support from the people, a primary maxim expounded by Mao Tse-tung.

The failure of the 20th August and 30th September (1955) demonstrations brought home to the FLN leaders the fact that they had somehow missed out an essential part of the insurgent blue-print. This omission was hastily rectified, and in December (1955) a three-month campaign was launched to win the minds of the people, during which insurgent cadres went amongst the villagers preaching and exhorting. At first terror and intimidation were combined with verbal persuasion, but gradually the former two elements were decreased until by the spring of the following year (1956) the FLN had the approbation, if not yet the willing active support, of the majority of the Muslim population, and by mid-1956 this had developed into a revolutionary mass movement throughout most of Algeria.

Until December 1955, the French might have been able to drive a wedge between the FLN (which until then had only antagonized and frightened the people) and the Muslim masses, but they missed this golden opportunity. It was not until November 1957 that the 5th Bureau was established and allowed to start work on the minds of the Muslims in the country. Then it was far too late.

The first years of the Algerian War consisted of a three-cornered fight between the French Army, the FLN and the MNA. Later, when the French Army and the Europeans became politically and violently involved against their own

Government and each other, the conflict became less simple. The bitter, underground struggle between the FLN and the MNA absorbed much of the vicious energy that might otherwise have been available for use against the French Army. The question is: how much? Undoubtedly it handicapped the insurgent effort considerably, but it would be over-optimistic to suggest that it might ever have been sufficient to swing the scale the other way. The French Army's task might have been harder, but from a military point of view French strategy and tactics would still have been able to smother any extra effort the insurgents might have been capable of mustering.

There is misconception and argument over the degree of Communist influence on the course of the Algerian insurrection. The French authorities insist that it was great, that Communist aid was given in quantity and that France, by combating the insurrection, was fighting the NATO Cold War battle against the Soviet Union on the southern flank. This is exaggerated, although it is very true that Communists everywhere like to fish in other people's troubled waters. Communist influence barely touched the FLN war effort.

The FLN — and also indeed the MNA — had strong traces of the Communist imprint on their organization and methods, and several of the leaders were either former Communists or well versed in Communist techniques, which inclined many to think that these two revolutionary bodies were Communist inspired or dominated. The methods may have been similar, but the aims were completely different. The FLN was, without a shadow of doubt, a nationalist body, fighting simply and solely for complete independence, harnessing the Prophet Mohammed rather than Karl Marx to its cause. Although it never scrupled to use Communist assistance, arms and money for its ultimate objective, this attitude was inflexibly maintained throughout. Neither Communism nor Communists made the slightest impact on the FLN, but on the contrary were selfishly exploited by it. The FLN outsmarted the Communists all along the line by taking all it could from them, and then playing them off at their own game.

The FLN would not allow Communists to join unless they forswore their former allegiances, and then they entered strictly as individuals. 'Block membership', either Communist or MNA, was not tolerated at all, and any attempts of Communists within the FLN to group together to push their own political creed were ruthlessly crushed. The FLN exploited the Communists on every possible occasion and, for example, used PCA members to help it manufacture or obtain explosives and teach it to use them. It took over the PCA 'back street' arsenal as soon as it could. In 1955, when the PCA came out openly on the side of the FLN and the insurrection, there was some overt co-operation between the FLN in Algiers and the Maquis Rouge squads, but these Communist squads were cynically and deliberately expended on suicide missions until they ceased to exist. After this the Communists had no success whatever in penetrating the FLN.

In France, Communist influence on the Algerian War was overrated, but agitation by French Communists, including Deputies, against the way the French Army was dealing with the insurrection, embarrassed and depressed French soldiers. Communist political power in France, discredited by the Hungary Rising, was considerably reduced after 1956, and in the November 1958 elections Communist representation was reduced from 145 seats to a mere 10 in the National Assembly. This indicated the wane of Communist influence in France.

Let us now briefly consider the French side of the picture. Involved in insurrection in both Morocco and Tunisia, the French were taken by surprise by the outbreak of war, as Algeria had been so quiet for so long. Thinking it was a tribal rising, instigated by political agitators, plus a little opportune banditry and paying off old tribal scores, the French Army moved against the trouble spots in a traditional punitive manner. For many months there was a welter of confused rebellion by the ALN (with some Algerian Muslim nationalist leaders denouncing it), inter-tribal fighting and depredations by bandits and smugglers, so the French may be forgiven for their deduction.

Still thinking that economic and social evils and neglects were the cause of the outbreak, the French built blockhouses in troubled regions, sent out strong fighting patrols, dispatched small mobile columns and carried out cordon-and-search operations, all of which had limited success owing to shortage of sufficient troops to carry out these measures effectively. Only slowly, as troops returned from the Indo-China theatre, did the strength of the French Army in Algeria rise from about 60,000 to 100,000. Also, it was six months before a state of emergency was declared: another restricting factor that helped the ALN to survive.

Once the true situation became apparent, reservists were recalled and conscripts employed in Algeria. The strength of the French forces there increased to about 250,000 by the spring of 1956, and then to over 400,000. With these numbers of troops available the quadrillage system, i.e. sitting heavily on the population and communication centres, which kept the ALN units restlessly roaming the countryside when they would have dearly liked to be in the cities and towns, was reasonably successful. The quadrillage system lay like a wet blanket on the revolt, and choked its expansion. Other measures, such as moving whole sections of the population to divorce the insurgents from the people, and thus deprive them of intelligence, food and support, also hit very hard at the ALN. The Challe Plan, which freed more troops for a mobile role and rooted out much of the OPA and other supporting elements, proved to be the turning-point of the war. These measures beat the ALN in Algeria to a standstill.

The barriers on the Algerian frontiers were a far greater success than has been realized. Publicity was usually given to the few insurgents and small quantities of arms that got through, but less was said about the thousands of armed and trained ALN soldiers who were forced to remain in helpless idleness because they were physically unable to enter Algeria.

Although claiming, and at times practising, a right of pursuit over the frontiers, the French stuck to the rules—with one or two much publicized exceptions, such as the bombing of

Sakiet—respecting the international borders, but the temptation to cross them in force to destroy the ALN troops in the Eastern and Western Bases, which the French Army was quite capable of doing in a swift operation, must have been overwhelming. Not enough is made of French restraint in this matter. Such an action might have caused international repercussions, but it would probably also have destroyed the conventional part of the ALN, which could never have been reconstituted and re-armed.

Once the situation was appreciated and once sufficient troops were available, French counter-insurgent strategy was good, succeeding in almost defeating the ALN in the field in Algeria. Had not other disrupting events, such as the European Insurrection, the Generals' Revolt and the rise of the OAS occurred, the remnants of the ALN would have merely provided a 'live hare' for the French Army to hunt, as was the case in the latter stages of the Malayan Communist Insurrection.

The French Army's main weakness in a war of this type was its complement of Algerian Muslim soldiers and auxiliaries, who were fair game for terrorism and intimidation by the FLN. The French officers tended to place too much faith in them, refusing to believe that they would not remain loyal, despite subversive persuasion, which often proved to be too strong. The desertion rate was consistently high, and several too-trusting French officers were murdered by their Muslim soldiers who deserted with their arms to the ALN. Of the some 180,000 Algerian Muslims in French Army service in 1954, only about 40,000 remained at the end of the war, a hard core that stayed only because the alternative was certain death and torture at the hands of their countrymen.

Although late in the field with psychological warfare, French officers had learnt in Indo-China many hard lessons, which they attempted to apply in Algeria. Some of their efforts at 'brainwashing' Muslims in internment camps and regroupment centres were frighteningly successful. They had some success also in persuading turncoats to return and betray their former comrades, and managed to bribe groups of the MNA and the ALN to fight for a time on the Government side. But the 5th

Bureau officers became immersed in politics, and misdirected their efforts, becoming deeply involved in the revolts that shook Algiers, and all France as well.

The French Army, meaning strictly speaking the regular officer cadre, had gradually assumed, in the absence of strong French government, a unique position of authority and prestige, and it became convinced that its mission was to save Algeria for France. Most French officers believed that French politicians had betrayed them in Indo-China, and were apprehensive lest the same occur in Algeria. For a while the Army preached integration of Muslim and European within a French Algeria, a policy at variance to that of the Europeans—but then the Army was remote from the Europeans and never really got into rapport with them. However, many army officers were con-converted, or became sympathetic, to the Europeans' aims and policies during and just before the European Insurrection of January 1960.

The Army was hurt and resented President de Gaulle's attitude towards it after his return to power, and once it saw that he was prepared to grant some form of independence to Algeria, many officers became bitter and disillusioned. The Generals' Revolt of April 1961 discredited the Army completely, a fact that gave hope to the exhausted ALN in the field in Algeria, encouraging it to hang on grimly for a little longer.

Handicapped as it was by an inward complex caused by previous defeats, the French Army did magnificent work in Algeria during the early years of the insurrection right up until 1960, beating the ALN in the military struggle. This record of achievement was overshadowed by its later dubious political activities and intrigues which helped the FLN to win the political battle.

The third power in Algeria was the European community which, living in a world of its own, disdainful of the Muslims, out of touch with the French Army and remote from the pulse of France, had over the years been able to veto many unpopular political measures. In February 1956, the Europeans had pelted the Prime Minister, Mollet, with tomatoes; when General

Catroux's appointment as Governor-General was cancelled at their insistence, they gained an inflated idea of their own authority and importance. Suspecting that the successive French Governments were either secretly negotiating—or about to negotiate—with the FLN, the Europeans became more restless, discontented and vocal as the months went by.

The Ultras felt they had been used in some way they could not quite define by the Gaullists and the Army in the series of events in May 1958 which resulted in the return of de Gaulle to power, and, like the Army, they bitterly resented his later attitude towards them. Ultra terrorism increased as they saw how he was handling the Algerian problem. Rather late in the day, the Europeans tried to enlist the support of the Army, but only partly succeeded. The officers were suspicious and on their dignity, while the bulk of the Army consisted of unwilling conscripts and discontented recalled reservists, who had a poor opinion of the Europeans. At the best the Europeans and the Army were uneasy allies in adversity. Towards the end of the war the OAS embarked upon tactics of despair, which destroyed any remaining world sympathy.

The West, and America in particular, dedicated to supporting majority democratic rule in Africa, were anxious lest the European majority seize power from a weak French Government, and establish an independent state with a white minority rule, as in South Africa. Although unpopular with America because of his reluctance to co-operate wholeheartedly with NATO, President de Gaulle received American support, especially at the time of the Generals' Revolt, for this very reason. This fear may also have been largely the reason why America would not openly and unequivocally back the FLN, lest this course abruptly project the Europeans into seizing power in Algeria. As de Gaulle clipped power from the Europeans, their potential in this respect declined.

What were the prospects of the Europeans seizing independent power in Algeria? Until 1958, they may have had a fair chance of producing a *fait accompli* that would have been difficult to reverse, had they been politically united and better organized, owing to the weak, muddled state of the successive French governments. Had the Europeans wooed the Army at an early stage and won its support, they would have been able to seize power, but the moment passed when de Gaulle became the Prime Minister. No shrewd, far-seeing leader of any stature arose to unite the Europeans, who were too easily swayed by the emotions of the moment to adhere rigidly to any cold, calculated long-term plan to achieve power, such as was being followed by the FLN.

The question is often posed as to how important were the new-found natural resources of the country, and how they affected the insurrection. The discovery of oil in Algeria in 1956, and subsequently of other natural resources in quantity, gave great economic value to an otherwise poor agricultural country, but the sight of these riches merely made the protagonists more single-minded and determined, as they simply added glitter to the ultimate prize. In itself, oil hardly affected the course of the fighting, but it was a strong weapon in the hands of the Provisional Algerian Government as a bargaining counter.

The key figure from 1958 onwards was President de Gaulle, who towered above all others, and whose patience, immense prestige and political acumen finally brought about a cease-fire. Before he returned to power the situation in both Algeria and France was going from bad to worse. Civil war in France was not far below the surface. On taking up office as Prime Minister he curtailed the political power of the Army and the Europeans, and then set to work to settle the war in Algeria on the best possible terms he could get for France.

As a first step he tried to create a body of moderate Algerian Muslim politicians by instituting fairly honest (for Algeria at the time) elections, but FLN intimidation and terrorism nullified this move. Realizing that he could not reach past the FLN, de Gaulle then made his offer of the Peace of the Brave. When this was refused he knew he would have to make concessions, so after a discreet interval secret contacts were made between the French Government and the FLN.

These gave him little hope of being able to placate the FLN

with offers of limited autonomy under French sovereignty, so, anxious to cut his losses and bring the war to an end, he began to pave the way to giving Algeria complete independence by offering, in September 1959, a choice that included secession. Overcoming with difficulty majority French opinion and distaste, open talks were arranged with the FLN. After the Generals' Revolt, which projected talks caused, de Gaulle saw that the situation was politically hopeless, although the military battle had been almost won by the French Army, so he hurried negotiations through as fast as he could. President de Gaulle was the statesman to whom the FLN owe much in their struggle to achieve independence for Algeria.

In conclusion one can say briefly that from a military point of view the war in Algeria was lost by the insurgents, but that they won it by political and diplomatic means. It showed that both political and military capabilities in a struggle of this nature must be closely linked together, so that varying pressures from one or both can be asserted as the situation demands. In the earlier years of the Algerian Insurrection military pressures and activities were more apparent and necessary, while in the later stages the political aspect assumed greater importance, but both combined and co-ordinated efforts were essential throughout, and without either one or the other the insurgents would have lost the war.

Acknowledgements

Many works have been consulted during the compilation of this book, and grateful acknowledgement is made in particular to the authors, contributors, or editors of the following, which have added immensely to my own knowledge and experience.

Aimée et Souffrante: Algérie by Jacques Soustelle (Paris: Plon, 1956).

Algerian ABC by Tanya Mathews (Geoffrey Chapmen, 1961).

Algerian Problem (The) by Edward Behr (Hodder & Stoughton, 1961).

Algerian Rebellion and Revolution (The) by Joan Gillespie (Praegar: New York, 1960).

Barricades et Colonels by Serge and Merry Bromberger, Georgette Elgey, and Jean-François Chauvel (Paris: Fayard, 1960).

Case Studies in Insurgency and Revolutionary Warfare: Algeria 1954–1962 by Paul a Jureidini (American University: Washington, 1963).

De Gaulle et l'Algérie by Louis Terrenoire (Paris: Fayard, 1964).

Guerres Insurrectionelles et Révolutionnaires by G. C. M. Bonnet (Paris: Payot, 1958).

La Guerre d'Algérie by Jules Roy (Paris: Juilliard, 1960).

La Guerre Moderne by Roger Trinquier (Paris: Le Table Ronde, 1961).

L'Algérie et la Rébellion by Raymond Aron (Paris: Plon, 1957).

La Nuit Coloniale by Ferhat Abbas (Paris: Juilliard, 1962).

La Question by Henri Alleg (Paris: Editions de Minuit, 1958).

La Révolution Algérienne by Charles-Henri Favrod (Paris: Plon, 1959).

ACKNOWLEDGEMENTS

La Révolution Algérienne by Francis Jeanson (Milan: Feltrinelli Editore, 1962).

La Révolution du 13 Mai by Alain de Serigny (Paris: Plon, 1958).

L'Armée d'Algérie et la Pacification by Michel Deon (Paris: Plon, 1959).

La Tragédie Algérienne by Raymond Aron (Paris: Plon, 1957).

Le FLN et Algérie by Charles-Henri Favrod (Paris: Plon, 1962).

Le Malaise de l'Armée by Jean Planchais (Paris: Plon, 1958).

Le Procès d'Edmond Jouhaud (Compte rendu sténographique) (Paris: Editions Albin Michel, 1962).

Le Procès de Raoul Salan (Compte rendu sténographique) (Paris: Editions Albin Michel, 1962).

Les Français d'Algérie by Pierre Nora (Paris: Juilliard, 1961).

Les Origines de la Guerre d'Algérie by Robert Aron (Paris: Fayard, 1962).

Les Rebelles Algériens by Serge Bromberger (Paris: Plon, 1957).

Les 13 Complots du 13 Mai by Merry and Serge Bromberger (Paris: Fayard, 1959).

Lieutenant in Algeria by Jean-Jacques Servan-Schreiber (Hutchinson, 1958).

Mes Combats by Joseph Ortiz (Paris: Editions Pensée Modern, 1964).

Nous Avons Pacifié Tazalt by Jean-Yves Alquier (Paris: Robert Laffont, 1957).

Ordeal in Algeria by Richard and Joan Brace (D. Van Nostrand Co. Inc.: New York, 1960).

St Michael and the Dragon by Pierre Leulliette (Heinemann, 1964).

Struggle for Algeria (The) by Joseph Kraft (Doubleday Co. Inc.: New York, 1961).

The Test: De Gaulle and Algeria by C. L. Sulzberger (Rupert Hart-Davis, 1962).

Tragedy in Algeria by Gerard Mansell (Oxford University Press, 1961).

Throat-Cutters (The) by Benoist Rey (John Calder, 1961).

War in Algeria by Tanya Mathews (Fordham University Press: USA, 1961).

Index

The following words and sets of initials are not included in the Index as they appear on the majority of pages:

Algeria(n)(s)
ALN
Arab(s)
European(s)
FLN
France
French
French Army

P   225

Index

Pakistan, 123
Pan-Arab(ism)(ist), 30, 33, 37
Paris, 28, 29, 76, 77, 85, 93, 103–105, 107–113, 127, 128, 131, 138, 140, 141, 146, 148, 150, 151, 156, 157, 159, 170, 171, 174–180, 183
PCA, 27, 28, 33, 36, 39, 40, 54, 56, 58, 59, 203, 214
Peace of the Brave, 129, 137, 140, 196, 219
Peking, 159, 160
Petain, Marshal, 103
Petit, General, 175, 181
Pflimlin, Pierre, 102–104, 106, 107, 109, 111, 113
Philippeville, 94, 135, 174
Philippines, 9
Phoenicians, 19
Poland, 82, 139
Pope, 20
Popular Front, 29, 30
PPA, 30–34, 37, 85
Provisional Executive, 195, 196, 199, 200
Provisional Government (of the OAS), 197
Psychological Warfare (also see 5th Bureau), 95
Provisional Algerian Government (of FLN), 123, 125, 130, 140–143, 154–156, 159–161, 167, 168, 173, 189, 190, 192, 193, 200, 204, 219

Quadrillage (system), 64, 78, 131, 132, 206, 215
Querville, Admiral, 171, 172, 180

Rabat, 67, 130
Radio Algiers, 171, 193
Radio France, 171
Rafa, Colonel, 192
Red Cross, 98, 99, 126, 127, 138
Red Hand, 139
Reggan, 154
Reghala, 149, 171

Relizane, 92
Resident Minister (of Algeria), 67, 76, 80, 83, 96, 106, 114
Revolution(ary), French, 21
RFMA, 30, 31
RFP, 101
Rocher-Noir, 196
Rome(n)(s), 19, 195
Rumania, 139

Saadi, Yecef, 80, 81
Safeguard Commission, 97, 126, 138
Sahara(n) (Desert), 21, 43, 44, 79, 90, 92, 109, 130, 154, 168, 169, 172, 178, 189, 190, 191, 195
Saharan Front, 94
Saida, 121, 122, 133, 175
Saida Mountains, 130
Said Mohammed, 85, 121, 142
Saint-Hellier, General, 170, 171
Sakiet, 98–100, 102, 127, 204, 216
Salan, General, 83, 84, 105–112, 114, 125, 127, 128, 131, 149, 159, 162, 169, 171, 173, 175, 178, 180, 181, 186, 187, 193, 197, 198
Santé Prison, 138
SAS, 95
SAU, 95
Saudi Arabia, 94
Second African Conference, 122
Security Services, 153
Seine, 127
Senegal, 25
Setif, 33, 156
Si Azzedine, 125
Si Cherif, 96
Sid Cara, 110
Sidi Bel Abbes, 44, 177
Si Haoues, 133
Simon, General, 170, 173
Souk-Ahras, 92, 119
Soummam Conference, 70–72, 74, 79, 81, 89, 204, 207

229